Gothick Architecture

A Reprint of the Original 1742 Treatise

Batty Langley

and

Thomas Langley

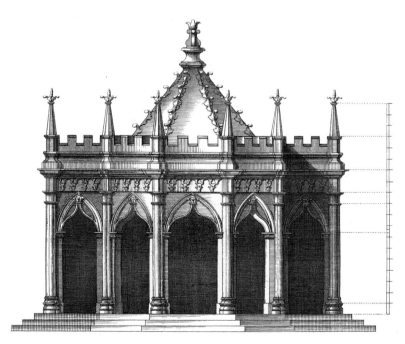

DOVER PUBLICATIONS, INC.
Mineola, New York

Bibliographical Note

This Dover edition, first published in 2003, is an unabridged republication of the work originally published in 1742 in England under the title, *Ancient Architecture Restored, and Improved, by A Great Variety of Grand and Useful Designs, Entirely New in the Gothic Mode for the Ornamenting of Buildings and Gardens.*

DOVER *Pictorial Archive* SERIES

Library of Congress Cataloging-in-Publication Data

Langley, Batty, 1696-1751.
    [Ancient architecture]
    Gothick architecture : a reprint of the original 1742 treatise : with 64 plates / Batty Langley and Thomas Langley.—Dover ed.
        p. cm.— (Dover pictorial archive series)
    Originally published: Ancient architecture. [London : s.n.], 1742.
    ISBN 0-486-42614-9 (pbk.)
     1. Architecture—England—Details—Pictorial works—Early works to 1800. 2. Gothic revival (Architecture)—England—Pictorial works—Early works to 1800. 3. Architecture—England—18th century—Pictorial works—Early works to 1800. I. Langley, T. (Thomas), 1702-1751. II. Title. III. Series.

NA2840 .L195 2003
720'.942'0903—dc21

                            2002041029

Manufactured in the United States of America
Dover Publications, Inc., 31 East 2nd Street, Mineola, N.Y. 11501

ANCIENT

ARCHITECTURE,

Reſtored, and Improved, by
A Great Variety of GRAND and uſefull DESIGNS,

Entirely New

In the *GOTHICK* MODE

For the Ornamenting of
BUILDINGS and *GARDENS*

Exceeding every Thing thats Extant.

Exquiſitely Engraved

On *LXIV* large Quarto Copper-Plates

and printed on SUPERFINE Royal PAPER

By *BATTY* and *THOMAS LANGLEY*
of Meards Court Dean Street Soho

Price 15 Shillings in Sheets

Buildings *in general Surveyed.* Artificers Works *Measured and Valued.*
Eſtates *in Lands, or in Buildings, Plan'd.* Gardens, Parks *&c laid out &c*
Grottos, Caſcades, Temples, *&c Deſign'd and Built,* Plans *and* Views *of*
Buildings &c Engraved and Printed in the most Exquiſite Manner
By the Editors

TO HIS GRACE

CHARLES

DUKE OF

RICHMOND,

AND TO HIS GRACE

JOHN

DUKE OF

MONTAGU.

May it please Your GRACE'S.

My LORDS,

THE Encouragement of *Arts* and *Industry*, being YOUR GRACE's Delights; and this Specimen (or Attempt) for to reſtore the *Rules* of the ANCIENT SAXON ARCHI-TECTURE, (vulgarly, but miſtakenly called *Gothic*) which have been loſt to the Public for upwards of ſeven hundred Years paſt, being *Honoured* with YOUR GRACE's *Approbations*, and *Encouragements*; It is therefore moſt Humbly Inſcribed to YOUR GRACE's Protections,

By, my LORDS,

Your GRACE'S

moſt Dutiful and moſt Affectionate Frater,

BATTY LANGLEY.

T O T H E

DEAN and CHAPTER

O F T H E

Collegiate Church of St Peter Westminster.

Right *Rev.* and *Rev.* SIRS,

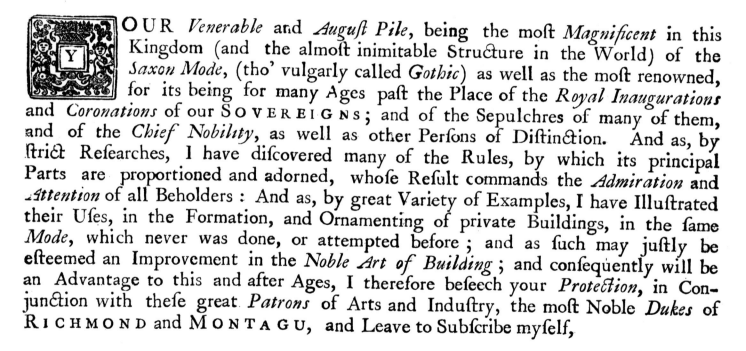 OUR *Venerable* and *August Pile*, being the most *Magnificent* in this Kingdom (and the almost inimitable Structure in the World) of the *Saxon Mode*, (tho' vulgarly called *Gothic*) as well as the most renowned, for its being for many Ages past the Place of the *Royal Inaugurations* and *Coronations* of our SOVEREIGNS; and of the Sepulchres of many of them, and of the *Chief Nobility*, as well as other Persons of Distinction. And as, by strict Researches, I have discovered many of the Rules, by which its principal Parts are proportioned and adorned, whose Result commands the *Admiration* and *Attention* of all Beholders : And as, by great Variety of Examples, I have Illustrated their Uses, in the Formation, and Ornamenting of private Buildings, in the same *Mode*, which never was done, or attempted before ; and as such may justly be esteemed an Improvement in the *Noble Art of Building* ; and consequently will be an Advantage to this and after Ages, I therefore beseech your *Protection*, in Conjunction with these great *Patrons* of Arts and Industry, the most Noble *Dukes* of RICHMOND and MONTAGU, and Leave to Subscribe myself,

Right *Rev.* and *Rev.* SIRS,

Your most Obedient

and most Humble Servant,

BATTY LANGLEY.

ENCOURAGERS

To the Reſtoring of the

SAXON ARCHITECTURE.

LORD *Hardwick*, Lord High Chancellor of *Great-Britain*.

The moſt Noble *Dukes of*

Richmond
Grafton
St *Albans*
Bolton
Devonſhire
Marlborough
Rutland
Montagu
Queenſberry
Newcaſtle
Portland
Argyll
Mancheſter
Buccleugh
Athol

The Right Honourable the *Earls of*

Lincoln
Weſtmoreland
Winchelſea and *Nottingham*
Cheſterfield
Cardigan
Carliſle
Shaftſbury
Litchfield
Holderneſs
Radnor
Rochford
Albemarle
Cholmondely
Loudon
Uxbridge
Pomfret
Earl *Fitzwalter*
Effingham
Harrington
Hertford
Tinley
Orrery
Arran
Inchiquin
Abercorne
Fitzwilliams

The Right Honourable the Lords *Viſcounts*

Fauconberg
Torrington
Windſor

The Right Reverend the Lords *Biſhops of*

Wincheſter
Rocheſter

The Right Honourable the *Lords*

Abergavenny
Clinton
North and *Guildford*
Petre
Brooke
Ward
Carteret
Gower
Conway
Foley
Walpole
Hobart
Talbot
Montfort
Ilcheſter
Baltimore
Gallway
Archibald Hamilton
Glenorchy
Dunmore
The Right Honourable the Lady *Germain*
The Honourable Miſs *Edwards*
The Right Honourable the Marquiſs of *Carnarvon*
The Right Honourable the Lord Chief Juſtice *Lee*
The Right Honourable the Lord Chief Juſtice *Willes*
Mr. Juſtice *Wright*
Mr. Juſtice *Burnet*
Mr. Juſtice *Parker*
Mr. Juſtice *Chapple*
Mr. Juſtice *Forteſcue*
Mr. Baron *Reynolds*
Mr. Baron *Abney*

The Right Honourable Arthur *Onſlow*, Eſq;
The Right Honourable St *Conyers D'Arcy*
The Right Honourable *Horatio Walpole* Eſq;
The Hon. General *Churchill*
Sir *Watkin Williams Wynne*
Sir *Thomas Frankland*
Sir *James Gray*
Sir *William Clayton*
Sir *John Peachy*
Sir *Francis Daſhwood*
Sir *James Daſhwood*
Sir *Henry Lyddel*
Sir *William Irby*
Sir *Michael Newton*
Sir *Robert Saliſbury Cotton*
The Right Honourable *Horatio Walpole*, Junior, Eſq;
The Hon. *William Finch*, Eſq;
George Dodington, Eſq;
Henry Fox, Surveyor of his Majeſty's Works, Eſq;
Richard Williams, Eſq;
William Vaughan, of Merioneth, Eſq;
John Campbel, of Stackpole Court in the County of *Pembroke*, Eſq;
Robert Vyner, Eſq;
—— *Northy*, Eſq;
Thomas Duncomb, Eſq;
James Brown, Eſq;
William Criſpe, Eſq;
—— *Carter*, Eſq;
The Reverend Dr. *Kenrick*
Mr *Tho. Hinton*, Deputy Surveyor
Mr *Thomas Grant*, Clerk of the Works
Mr *William Booth*, Deputy Maſon
Mr *John Bacchus*, Carpenter
Mr *Henry Sims*, Smith

N. B. The five laſt belong reſpectively to St *Peter* at *Weſtminſter*.

Mr *Walter Cameron*, Carpenter
Mr *John Elder*, *Shilbottle*, *Northumberland*, Carpenter

DISSERTATION

On the ANTIQITY *of the Principal* ANCIENT BUILDINGS, *that have been, and now are in this Kingdom, by Way of Introduction to the following Work.*

THE RULES by which the ancient Buildings of this Kingdom were erected and adorned, having been entirely lost for many Centuries past; I therefore, for upwards of twenty Years, in order to reftore and publifh them for the Good of Pofterity, have affiduoufly employed myfelf, as Opportunities have happen'd, in making Refearches into many of the moft ancient Buildings, now ftanding in this Kingdom: And from thence to extract Rules for forming fuch Defigns and Ornaments in the ancient Mode, which will be exceeding beautiful in all Parts of private Buildings: And efpecially in *Rooms of State, Dining Rooms, Parlours, Stair-cafes,* &c. And in *Portico's, Umbrello's, Temples,* and *Pavillions* in *Gardens, Parks,* &c. of which I have given Specimens in the following Sheets, for the Approbation of impartial Judges.

UPON the ftricteft Enquiry into the Hiftories of this Kingdom, and into the Chronicles of paft Ages, it doth not appear that any Edifices were built by the *Goths,* in this Kingdom: Notwithftanaing, that every ancient Building, which is not in the *Grecian Mode,* is called a *Gothic Building,* as *Weftminfter Abbey,* &c. for according to Mr. *De Rapin Thoyra,* in his Hiftory of *England,* the *Goths* (who were alfo called *Jutes,* and *Wittes*) were originally *Itinerants* in *Germany:* Who, fome time before the *Saxons* came into *Britain,* united themfelves with the *Saxons,* and ever after looked upon themfelves as one and the fame People, and were in general called *Saxons.*

IN or about the Year 449, when the *Romans* had voluntarily left *Britain* (after having kept it 500 Years in Subjection) *Hengift* and *Horfa,* two *Saxon* Princes, at the Requeft of the *Britifh* King *Vortigern,* came here with nine thoufand *Saxons* to affift him againft the *Picts* and *Scots*; many of which, very probable, were real *Goths,* altho' called *Saxons,* as being united, and were the firft that came into *Britain.*

IN the Year 530, which was 83 Years after the coming of *Hengift,* and when the *Saxons* had made themfelves Mafters of the firft four Kingdoms of the *Heptarchy, Rapin* faith, great Numbers of *Goths* or *Jutes,* with their Families, came to *Britain,* and uniting with the *Saxons,* their Pofterity became *Saxons* alfo; fo that long before the Year 1017, when *Edmund* the laft King of the *Saxons* (before the *Danes*) died; with whom fell the Glory of the *Englifh Saxons,* which was 586 Years after the Arrival of *Hengift,* and 487 Years after the coming of the laft mentioned *Goths,* their Names and Country were obliterated, and every one called himfelf an ENGLISH SAXON.

AND 'tis very reafonable to believe, that as in all Ages of the *Saxon* Monarchy, there was no Diftinction of *Goths* from *Saxons,* but in general were called *Saxons*; that, therefore, all the Edifices raifed by them were in general called *Saxon* (and not *Gothic*) Buildings; altho' it was to be allowed, that the *Goths* firft taught the *Saxons* how to build.

WHAT the Kinds of Buildings were, which were ftanding in *Britain,* at the Time of the *Saxons* firft coming, which had been built by the *Britains* and *Romans,* we have no Account of in Hiftory; nor indeed, was it poffible we fhould, fince that the Art of Printing was then unknown; and confidering that the Devaftations made in *Britain,* by the *Saxons*

at firft, for the Space of 234 Years, to wit, from the Year 455 to 689, when *Cadwalladar,* the laft King of the *Britains,* loft the whole Kingdom; and then immediately afterward, for the further Space of 129 Years, whilft the *Saxon* Kings of the *Heptarchy* were ftriving among themfelves for Sovereignty, which ended in the Year 818, making 363 Years Depredations in the whole; when *Egbert* King of the *Weft-Saxons* reduced all the other to his Subjection, and became the firft *Saxon* fole King of *England*; were fo great, that all publick and private Buildings, which had been erected by the *Britains* and *Romans,* were laid in one common Ruin: Nothing being to be feen (faith *Gildas*) but Churches burnt down and deftroyed to the very Foundations (both *Goths* and *Saxons* being *Pagans,* at their firft coming here) and the Inhabitants extirpated by the Sword, and buried under the Ruins of their own Houfes.

FROM the Year 455, when the firft Kingdom of the *Heptarchy* (*Kent*) was began by *Hengift,* unto the Year 597, which was for the Space of 142 Years (when Chriftianity was firft received by the *Saxons*) all the *Saxons* were Idolators, and confequently, all their Buildings for Worfhip were *Pagan-Temples*; which afterward, as Chriftianity was received, were converted into Chriftian Churches.

ETHELBERT, the fifth King of *Kent,* was the firft *Saxon* King who was converted to Chriftianity; and who not only converted *Sebert,* but in the Year 605 he affifted him in Building of the Church of St. *Peter* in the Weft of *London,* in a Place called by the *Saxons, Thornez* or *Thorney,* from the firft Chriftian Church, which had been built there by *Lucius,* King of *Britain,* in the Year 183; being at the End of four hundred Years Ruin, (after the Perfecution under *Dioclefian*), overgrown with Bufhes, Thorns, &c. In this Place (faith *Sulcardus*) the Temple of *Apollo* ftood, at the Time when *Antonius Pius* was Emperor of *Rome,* and being afterward thrown down by an Earthquake, upon its Ruins, *Sebert* built the Church aforefaid which he dedicated to St *Peter,* as *Lucius* had done 422 Years before him.

ETHELBERT alfo affifted *Sebert,* about the Year 610, to build the Cathedral Church of St *Paul's London,* which formerly had been the Temple of *Diana,* tho' fome fay *Ethelbert* founded it himfelf.

DURING the laft 400 Years of the *Saxon* Monarchy, the *Saxons* built great Numbers of Cathedrals, Churches, Chappels, Abbeys, Monaftries, &c. which at length became Sacrifices to the *Danes,* who in the laft 224 Years miferably afflicted them; and particularly from the Year 979, to 1001, in which Time the Ravages committed by the *Danes* were fuch, that nothing was to be feen all over the Kingdom, but Murders, Conflagrations, Plundering, and other Devaftations; fo that in the Year 1017, when King *Edmund* was murder'd by *Edrick,* and *Canutus* had feized upon the whole Kingdom, and made himfelf the firft *Danifh* King of *England*; all the venerable Buildings, which the *Saxons* had raifed (St *Paul's* Cathedral I believe only excepted) were then, either lying in their frightful Ruins, or fo irreparably defaced, that very little Judgement could be formed of what they had ever been.

BY this unhappy Conqueft, Pofterity was deprived, not only of the *Saxon Modes or Orders of Architecture,* but alfo,

of

of the Geometrical Rules, by which their Buildings in general were defigned, fet out, erected, and adorned; for it cannot be fuppofed, but that there were many ingenious *Saxon* Architects in thofe Times, who had compofed Manufcripts of all their valuable Rules, which, with themfelves, were deftroyed, and buried in Ruin; and therefore, notwithftanding, that all Buildings afterward erected might have a Similitude of the *Saxon Mode*; yet 'tis much to be doubted, if any of them ever came up to that *Beauty of Order*, which, 'tis very reafonable to believe, was contained in the *Saxon* Architecture.

Now as I have thus fhewn that the Pofterity of the *Goths*, by their Union, became *Englifh Saxons*; and that the *Saxon* Buildings were entirely ruined and defaced by the *mercylefs Danes*; 'tis therefore evident, that none of the ancient Buildings now ftanding in this Kingdom, which have been erected fince the *Danifh* Conqueft, are real *Gothic* (or *Saxon*) Buildings, as they are commonly called.

The principal Buildings that have been erected in this Kingdom from the Beginning of the *Danifh* Monarchy, to wit the Year 1017, unto the Reign of King *James* the firft, when *Inigo Jones* lived, who I think was the firft Perfon that introduced the *Grecian* Architecture in *England*, are the following, viz.

In the Time of the *Danifh* Government, which continued but 26 Years, *Canutus* built the Church of *Afhdon* in *Effex*; the Abbey of St *Benet* in *Norfolk*, and a ftately Church and Monaftery at St *Edmundfbury*; but *Hardicanute*, the third and laft *Danifh* King, (*Dane* like) inftead of erecting Buildings to his Memory, burnt the City of *Worcefter*.

King Edward, called the Confeffor, came to the Crown in the Year 1043, or 1044, and died in 1066. This King rebuilt the Church of St *Peter* at *Weftminfter*, and a Convent adjoining, which *Sebert* had before erected, and was afterward deftroyed by the *Danes*; he alfo new-built St *Margaret*'s Church at *Weftminfter* where it now ftands; before which Time, it ftood adjoining to the South Cloyfter of the old Abbey; part of which is now ftanding; and as 'tis very reafonable to believe, that, that Building was alfo built by *Sebert* at the Time when he built the Church of St *Peter*, or very foon afterward, therefore the Remains which now are ftanding muft be upwards of eleven hundred Years old.

In the Reign of William the Conqueror, who began in the Year 1067, and died 1087, the Abbeys, at *Battel* in *Suffex*, at *Selby* in *Yorkfhire*, at St *Saviours* in *Southwark*; the Priory of St *Nicholas* at *Exeter*; and the Town of *Newcaftle* on *Tyne*, were founded; the Foundation of St *Paul's* Cathedral began, after having been burnt by Lightning; the white Tower of the *Tower of London* in 1078, the *Minfter* at *York*, after having been burnt by the *Danes*; the Caftles at *Oxford*, *Exeter*, *Nottingham*, *York*, *Lincoln*, *Huntingdon* and *Cambridge*, and the new Church at *Salifbury*, were all built; and the Caftle of *Warwick* repaired.

In the Reign of William the Second, who began in the Year 1087, and died in 1100, the Abbeys at *Shrewfbury*, *Merton* in *Surry*, at *Lewes* in *Suffex*, the Hofpital of St *Leonard* at *York*, the Monaftery at *Norwich*; the Cathedral of *Salifbury*, and *Univerfity College* in *Oxford* were founded. The Cathedral Church of *Lincoln*, began. The Abbey at *Wenlock*; a *Fort* at *Newcaftle*; a Caftle at *Ledes* in *Kent*; a new Wall about the Tower of *London*, and a great Hall at *Weftminfter*, 270 Feet in Length, and 70 Feet in Breadth, were all built.

The City of *Carlifle*, which had been deftroyed by the *Danes*, and laid two Hundred Years in Ruin, was rebuilt.

London Bridge was alfo rebuilt with Timber, and the Abbey of St *Albans*, and the Church at *Rochefter* were repaired.

In the Reign of Henry I. who began in the Year 1100, and died in 1135, the Cathedral Church of *Exeter*, the Church of St *Mary Overy* in *Southwark*, the new Church and Cathedral at *Tewkfbury*, the Priories of *Dunftable*, of the *Holy Trinity*, now called *Chrifts Church London*, of St *Bartholomew*, and its Hofpital in *Smithfield*; of *Kenelworth*, of *Norton* in *Chefhire*, of *Merton*, and of *Ofney* near *Oxford*. The Abbeys of *Cirencefter*, *Reading*, *Thirbourn*, *Cumbermere*; *New Abbey* without *Winchefter*; and of *Merival* in *Warwickfhire*: The Monaftery of St *John* at *Colchefter*; of St *Andrew* at *Northampton*; and of *Plimpton* in *Devonfhire*; the Houfe of St *John of Jerufalem*, near *Smithfield*; the College of St *Mary* in the Town of *Warwick*, and the Hofpitals of *Kepar*, and of St *Crofs* near *Winchefter*, were all founded. The Priory of St *James* in *Briftol*; the Caftles of *Briftol*, *Cardiffe*, *almefbury*, *Shirbourn*, *Windfor*, and *Baynard* in *London*. The *Devifes* in *Wilts*; the *ftately Church at Salifbury*: And the Stone-bridges at *Bow*, and *Stratford* in *Effex*; (which were the firft Stone-bridges in *England*) were all built, and the Abbey of *Kenfham*, and Caftle of *Norham* upon the Banks of the *Tweed* were began.

In the Reign of King Stephen, who began in the Year 1135, and died in 1154, the Abbeys, of *Cogfhall* in *Effex*, of *Furneys* in *Lancafhire*, of *Harquilers* and *Feverfham* in *Kent*; of *Stratford Langthorn* near *London*; of *Boxley* in *Kent*; of *Non-Eaton*, in *Warwickfhire*. of *Filtey*, of *Rieval*, of *Newborough*, and *Beeland*, of *Kirkftead* in *Yorkfhire*, and many others, were founded; fo that more Abbeys (faith *Baker*) were erected in this King's Reign, than had been within the Space of a hundred Years before.

At *Heigham* in *Kent*, a Houfe for *Black Nuns*, and at *Carew*, a Houfe for *White Nuns*, were alfo founded; and the Hofpital of St *Katherine* by the Tower was new built.

In the Reign of Henry II. who began in the Year 1154, and died in 1189, the Abbey of *Bordefly*, and *Wigmore* Abbey, the Priories of *Dover*, and of *Bafinwork*, the Church of *Briftol*, (which *Henry VIII*. erected into a Cathedral) and the Caftle of *Rudlan*, and the *Stone-bridge* at *London*, were all founded. The Monaftery of St *Auguftine* in *Briftol*, of *Gorendon*, of *Leicefter*, (called St *Mary de Pratis*) of *Eaton*, and at *Glocefter*, the Caftle of *Anger* in *Effex*, and a new Timber-bridge at *London*, were all built: In the Year 1181, the *Temple Church* in *London* was finifhed; and in 1183 the Bifhop of *Canterbury*'s *Palace* at *Lambeth* was began.

In the Reign of Richard I. who began in the Year 1189, and died 1199, the *Tower-Wall* was new Built, and the Ditch made about it; a Monaftery at *Weft Durham* in *Norfolk* was founded; another was began at *Wolverhampton* in *taffordfhire*, and the *Collegiate Church* at *Lambeth* was finifhed.

In the Reign of King John, who began in the Year 1199, and died in 1216, the Abbeys of *Bowley* in the new Foreft in *Hampfhire*, and of the Black Monks in *Winchefter*, the Monaftery of *Farringdon*, and of *Hales-Owen* in *Shropfhire*, were founded. *Godftale* and *Wroxel* re-edified; the Chappel at *Knarefborough* enlarged, and the *Stone-Bridge* at *London* finifhed.

In the Reign of Henry III. who began in the Year 1216, and died in 1272, great Numbers of Abbeys, and St *Peter's College* in *Cambridge*, were founded. In the Year 1220, this King began the new Work of our Lady's Chappel at *Weftminfter*, where the Chappel of *Henry VII*. now ftands, and laid the firft Stone himfelf. In the Year 1245, he caufed the *Walls* and *Steeple* of the old Church of St *Peter* at *Weftminfter*, built by *Edward* the Confeffor, to be taken down; and enlarging the Church, caufed it to be new Built with greater Magnificence; which to effect, was the Work of the next 50 Years; at which Time its Weft-end came no further, than the firft Columns Weft from the Choir; all the Part from thence, together with the two old Towers, having been built fince, at the Expence of the Abbots of *Weftminfter*.

In

In the Year 1222, the Tower and Spire of St *Paul's*, which had been burnt down in 1087, was new built; the Stone Tower was 260 Feet from the Ground, to the Top of the Battlements, the Height of the Spire, above the Battlements, was 260 Feet more, making 520 Feet altitude, exclusive of the Ball and Crofs, which was near 20 Feet more.— A matchlefs Structure.—greatly exceeding all Buildings that have been fince raifed in this Kingdom. The *Savoy* was alfo built about the Year 1245.

In the Year 1260, the curious inlaid Floor or Pavement, yet remaining, of *Jafper Porphry, Lydian, Touchftone, Alabafter* and *Serpentine Stones*, was made before the high Altar in *Weftminfter* Abbey, at the Expence of *Richard de Ware*, an Abbot of *Weftminfter*, which is now 482 Years fince.

In the Reign of EDWARD I. who began in the Year 1272, and died in 1307, the Abbey of *Vale Royal* in *Chefhire* of the *Cifteaux Order*, and erton *College* in *Oxford*, were founded. *Baliol College* in *Oxford* was built, and the Church of St *Peter* at *Weftminfter* was nearly finifhed.

In the Reign of EDWARD II. who began in the Year 1307, and died in 1327, *Oriel College*, St *Mary-hall* in *Oxford*, and a Church of Fryers, in his *Manour* of *Langley*, were founded.

In the Reign of EDWARD III. who began in the Year 1327, and died in 1377, the Eaft-Minfter (an Abbey of the *Cifteaux Order*) near the Tower of *London*; *Kings-hall, Trinity-hall,* and *Pembroke-hall* in *Cambridge, Queens College, Exeter College*; *Hart-Hall,* and *Canterbury College* in *Oxford*, the *College* of *Cobham* in *Kent*, and the *Charter-houfe* near *Smithfield*, were all founded. The *Chappel* of St *Stephen* at *Weftminfter*, (which is now the *Houfe of Commons*) and St *Michaels Church*, near *Crooked Lane London*, were built; the *Chappel* at *Windfor* augmented, and the Caftle re-edified.

In this King's Reign, Abbot *Nicholas Litlington* built the *Hall, Jerufalem Chamber*, and the South and Weft Side of the great Cloifter, adjoining to *Weftminfter* Abbey; with the Granary and an adjoining Tower, which afterward was made the Dormitory for the *King's* Scholars.

In the Reign of RICHARD II. who began in the Year 1377, and died in 1399, *Trinity-hall* in *Cambridge*, the Gate-houfe to *Ely-houfe* in *Holbourn*, were new built; and *Weftminfter-hall*, with its ftately Porch, was rebuilt in the Year 1397.

In the Reign of HENRY IV. who began in the Year 1399, and died in 1413, a College at *Battlefield* in *Shropfhire*, a College at *Pomfret*; and a new College in *Winchefter*, were all founded. The *Guild-hall* in *London* was began in the Year 1411; the Stone-bridge at *Rochefter*, and *Newgate* in *London*, were built, the laft by *Richard Whittington*, Lord Mayor of *London*.

In the Reign of HENRY V. who began his Reign in the Year 1413, and died in 1422; *Bernards*, and *All-Souls Colleges* in *Oxford*, were founded.

In the Reign of HENRY VI. who began in the Year 1422, and died in 1460, the *College Royal*, and *Queens College* at *Cambridge, Eaton College* by *Windfor*, and *Mary Magdalene College* in *Oxford*, were all founded; and the Divinity-School in *Oxford*, the *College* of *Tatfhall* in *Lincolnfhire*, and *Leaden-hall* in *London* were built.

In the Reign of EDWARD IV. who began in the Year 1460, and died in 1483, he laid the Foundation of the new *Chappel* at *Windfor. London-Wall* was alfo built from *Cripplegate*, to *Bifhopfgate*; and *Bifhopfgate* was rebuilt alfo.

In the Reign of EDWARD V. and of RICHARD III. which began in the Year 1483, and ended in 1485, no Buildings of Note were erected.

In the Reign of HENRY VII. who began in the Year 1485, and died in 1508, *John Iflip* an Abbot of *Weftminfter*, in the Year 1500, built that Houfe, in which the *Dean of Weftminfter* now lives, and fet up the Statues of all the Kings and Queens, who had been Benefactors to that Church. The *Chappel* of our *Lady*, built at *Weftminfter* by HENRY III, was taken down in 1502, and a new Chappel of much greater Dimenfions was began to be built in its Place, with Stone, which is faid was brought from *Huddleftone Quarry* in *Yorkfhire*.

THIS Building, which is commonly called HENRY VIIth's Chappel, is of a quite different Mode, or Order of Architecture, from that of the *Abbey*, built by HENRY III. and indeed, the Invention of their Difference is much greater than is contained between any two of the *Grecian Orders*.

IT is a great Pity, that the Architect of this Chappel did not communicate to Pofterity the Rules by which it was erected and adorned, which he might very eafily have done, becaufe the Art of *Printing* had been then known for full thirty Years; and the firft *Printing* done in *England* was in an old *Chappel* of St *Ann*, then ftanding in the *Eleemofinary, Almnery*, or *Almory*, where anciently Alms were given (now corruptly called the *Ambry*) by *John Iflip*, aforefaid, who I believe was the Architect of this venerable Edifice, which *Leland* calls the Miracle of the World.

In this King's Reign, *Chrift's College, Jefus College*, and St *John's College* at *Cambridge*; *Corpus Chrifti College*, and *Brazen-nofe College* at *Oxford*; and the School of St *Paul's*, *London*, were all founded.

In the Reign of HENRY VIII. who began in the Year 1508, and died in 1547, *Chrift Church College* at *Oxford* was founded; *Hampton Court*, and *White-hall* (then called *York Place*) and the *Old Gate* near the *Tilt-yard* now belonging to the *Lord Falmouth*, and *Coventry Crofs* (in the Year 1542,) were all built.

In the Reign of EDWARD VI. who began in the Year 1547, and died in 1553, *Somerfet-houfe* was built by the Earl of *Hertford* in 1549.

In the Reign of MARY I. who began in the Year 1553, and died in 1558, St *John's College* in *Oxford* was built.

In the Reign of Queen ELIZABETH, who began in the Year 1558, and died in 1603, *Sidney College*, and *Emanuel College* in *Cambridge*, were founded; and the public Library at *Oxford* was built and furnifhed.

In the Reign of JAMES I. who began in the Year 1603, and died in 1625, *Hicks's-hall* near *Smithfield Bars*, and the *Banquetting-houfe* at *Whitehall*, were built—the laft by *Inigo Jones*.

NOW as it is very reafonable to believe that the *Modes* in which all thefe Buildings have been erected, the Banquetting Houfe excepted, were taken from Fragments, found among the *Saxon Ruins*; they may therefore be called *Saxon Buildings*; but why they have been called *Gothic*, I cannot account for.

AND as to continue the *Saxon Modes* of Building, under the *Gothic Appellation*, may be more agreeable and fooner underftood by many, than they would be, was I to call them *Saxon* as they actually are; therefore, all the following Defigns are called *Gothick*.

And as thefe *Modes of Building* have been and are condemned by many, on a Suppofition that their principal Parts have been put together, *without Rules or Proportion*; to prove that fuch is the Effect of want of Judgment, I have, in Plates A and B, as a Specimen of *the Beautiful Rules of the Ancients*, illuftrated the *Geometrical Plans* and *Elevations* of the *Bafes* and *Capitals*, to the two Varieties of Columns, now ftanding in *Weftminfter Abbey, viz.*

A 2   FIRST,

FIRST, those in the *Choir Part*, built by HENRY III. and those from the *Choir*, to the two Towers in the *West-End*, which were built afterward, by the *Abbots* of *Westminster*, as aforesaid, wherein every impartial Judge will see by Inspection, that their Members, both as to their Heights and Projectures, are determined and described with those beautiful Proportions, and Geometrical Rules, which are not excelled (if equalled) in any Parts of the *Grecian* or *Roman* Orders. Nor is that *Delicacy* and *Deception*, which is contained in these Columns, to be seen in any *Grecian* or *Roman* Columns, of the same Diameters. For, altho' these Columns in the West-part of the Abbey appear to be much *slenderer, weaker,* and of *less Diameter,* than the *Corinthian* Columns, in the *Portico* of St *Paul's* Cathedral (which are 4 Feet in Diameter) yet they are actually full 14 Inches more in their Diameters ; and consequently they are more than half as strong again. Because 16, the Square of the Diameter of one of St *Paul's* Columns, is less than two Thirds of 26, eight-twelfths, the Square of the Diameter of one of these Columns. *A Deception, not to be parallel'd, in all the Columns, yet erected, by both Greeks and Romans, in the whole World.*

IT is from these, and such like Researches, that I have extracted the Rules, and Proportions, by which all the Parts of the following Designs are adjusted ; and which, being in general made plain to Inspection, by the Scales of equal Parts affixed to each, needs no other Explication.

PLATE I, &c. to XVI. Contain five Varieties of Columns, with eleven Varieties of Entablatures, which are allowed by every impartial Judge to exceed all that have been done.

PLATE XVII, &c. to XXVIII. Contain 12 Varieties of Frontispieces for Doors, with their Members, geometrically described at large, never done before.

PLATE XXIX. Exhibits four Varieties of *Arcades* for *Piazza's,* with the Geometrical Construction of their Curves, never done before.

PLATE XXX. A *Saxon,* or ancient *Gothic* Colonade.

PLATE XXXI. An *Umbrello* in the *Saxon* Mode.

PLATE XXXII. A Gothic Portico, supposed to be, at the Entrance of a Banquetting Room, &c. of the same Mode.

PLATE XXXIII. Contains six Varieties of Circular Windows, or Lights to be placed over Doors, to illuminate Passages, &c.

PLATE XXXIV. Contains as many square Windows for Attic Stories, &c.

PLATE XXXV, &c. to XL. Contain six Varieties of Windows, for State-Rooms, Pavillions, &c.

PLATE XLI, &c. to XLVIII. Contain 8 Varieties of Chimney Pieces, not to be matched in the World.

PLATE XLIX, &c. to LXII. Contain fourteen Varieties of *Umbrello's, Temples,* and *Pavillions,* which are believed to come the nearest to the ancient *Saxon Architecture,* of all that has been done, since the *Danish* Conquest.

AND as this Specimen of my Endeavours to restore, and illustrate the Beauties of the *Saxon Architecture,* for the Good of Posterity, is *honoured* with the Encouragement of the preceding *Nobility* and *Gentry,* I make no Doubt, but that by their good Examples, all other *Lovers* and *Encouragers of Arts* and *Industry* will further encourage it ; that thereby I may be enabled, to communicate, in a *second Volume,* many other *useful Designs,* for *Cielling-Pieces, Insides of Rooms, Pavements, Stair Cases, Pagan Temples, Sylvan Towers, Saxon Tents, Niche's, Canopys, Monumental Pyramids,* &c. which I have extracted from the Works of the Ancients, and whose *Magnificence* and *Beauty* greatly excee all that have been done by both *Greeks* and *Romans.*

AND whereas it may be objected, that the Expence of these Kinds of Buildings will be greater, than Buildings of the same Magnitude in the *Grecian Mode* ; and especially by Workmen unable to perform them, I therefore give this public Notice, that I will undertake to erect all Sorts of Buildings in the *Saxon Mode* that may be required ; if free from Enrichments, for the same Expence, as a plain Building of the same Magnitude in the *Grecian Mode* would amount to ; and if enriched, for less Money than a Building of the same Magnitude in the *Grecian Mode* would come to ; being enriched with the common Ornaments used in any of the *Grecian Orders.*— And such *Noblemen* and Gentlemen who are pleased, may find all their own Materials, which will very greatly abate the Expence.

August 16th, 1742.

BATTY LANGLEY.

Plate **I.**

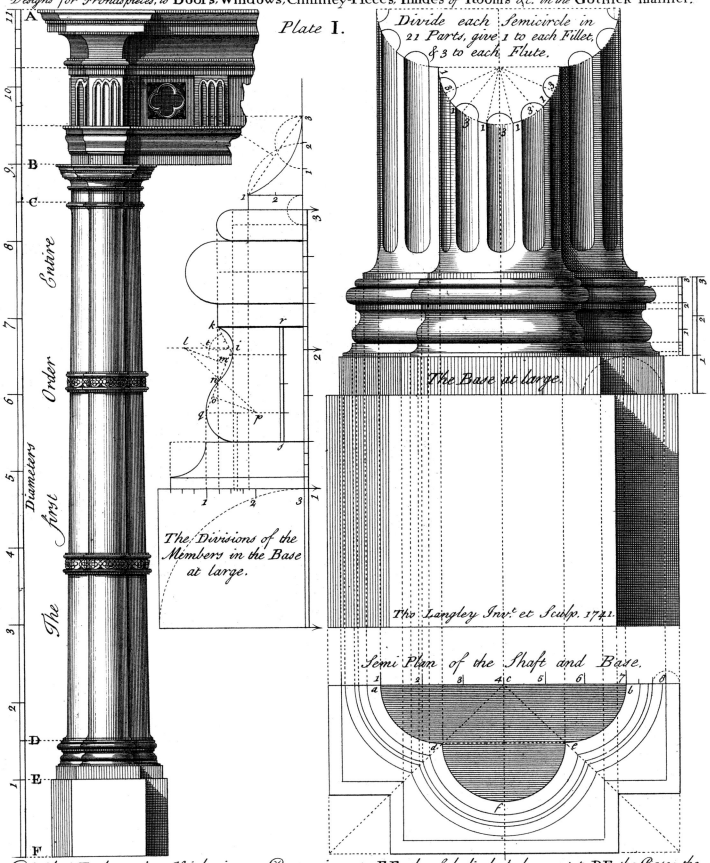

Divide each Semicircle in 21 Parts, give 1 to each Fillet & 3 to each Flute.

The Base at large.

The Divisions of the Members in the Base at large.

Tho. Langley Invt. et Sculp. 1741.

Semi Plan of the Shaft and Base.

Divide AF. *the entire Height into 11 Parts, give 1 to* EF. *the Subplinth, ½ the next to* DE. *the Base; the next 7 to* CD *the Shaft; the next ½ to* BC *the Capital, and the upper 2 to* AB *the Entablature.*

The Gothick Entablature & Capital, *of the first* Order *at large.*

Plate **II.**

Fig. I.

Fig. II.

Fig. III.

Fig. IV.

Batty and Thomas Langley Invent and Sculp. 1741.

A *Second* Gothick Entablature & Capital, *at large for* Order I.   *Plate* III.

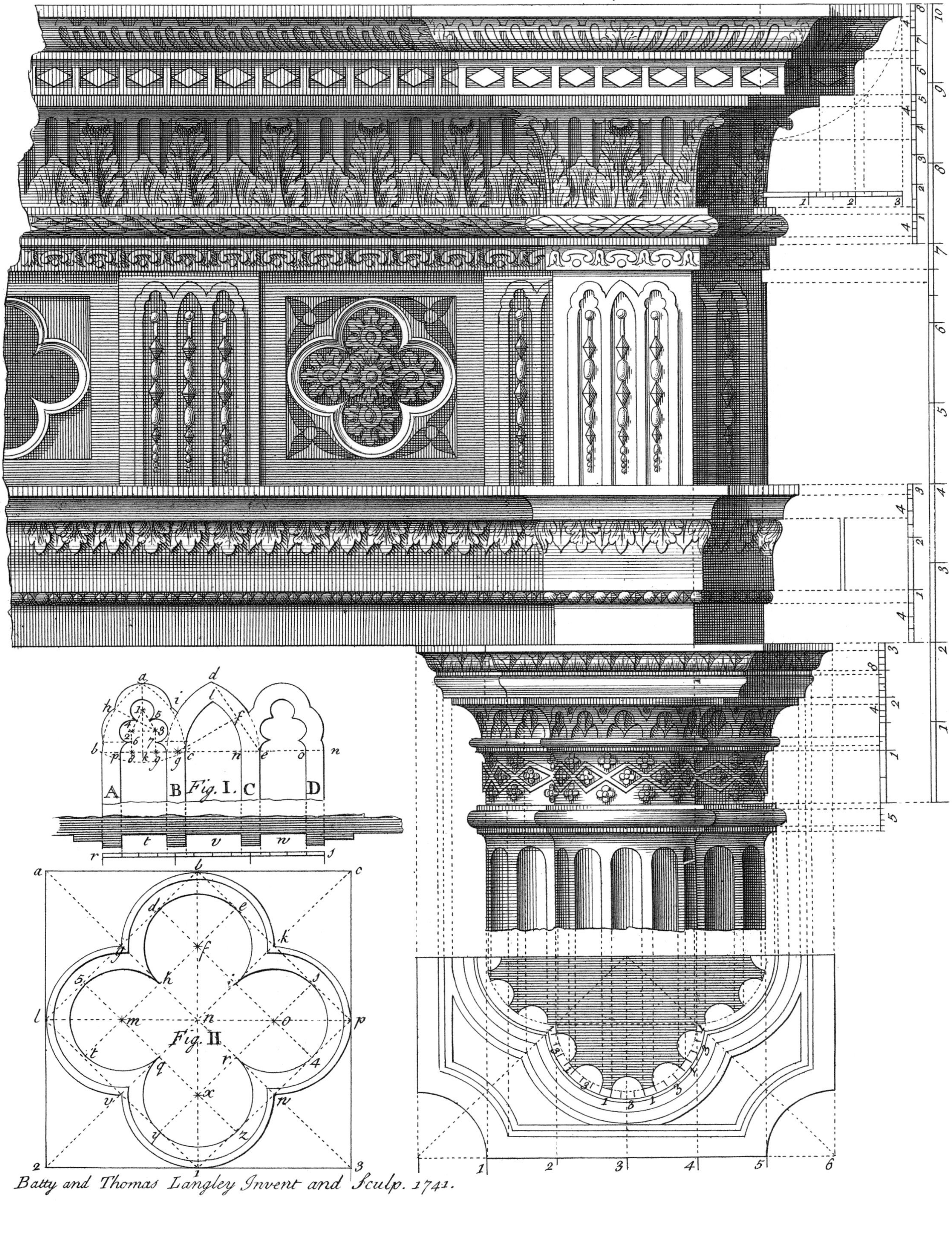

Fig. I.

A   B   C   D

Fig. II

Batty *and* Thomas Langley *Invent and Sculp.* 1741.

The Base at large

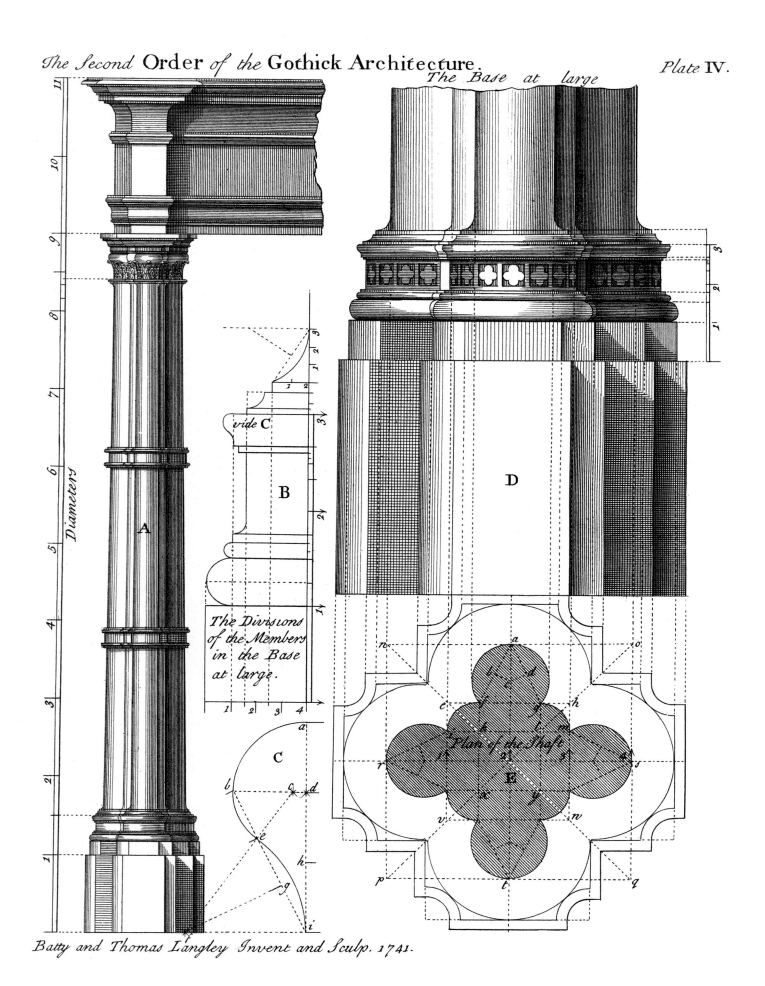

Diameters

A

vide C

B

The Divisions
of the Members
in the Base
at large.

C

D

Plan of the Shaft

E

Batty and Thomas Langley Invent and Sculp. 1741.

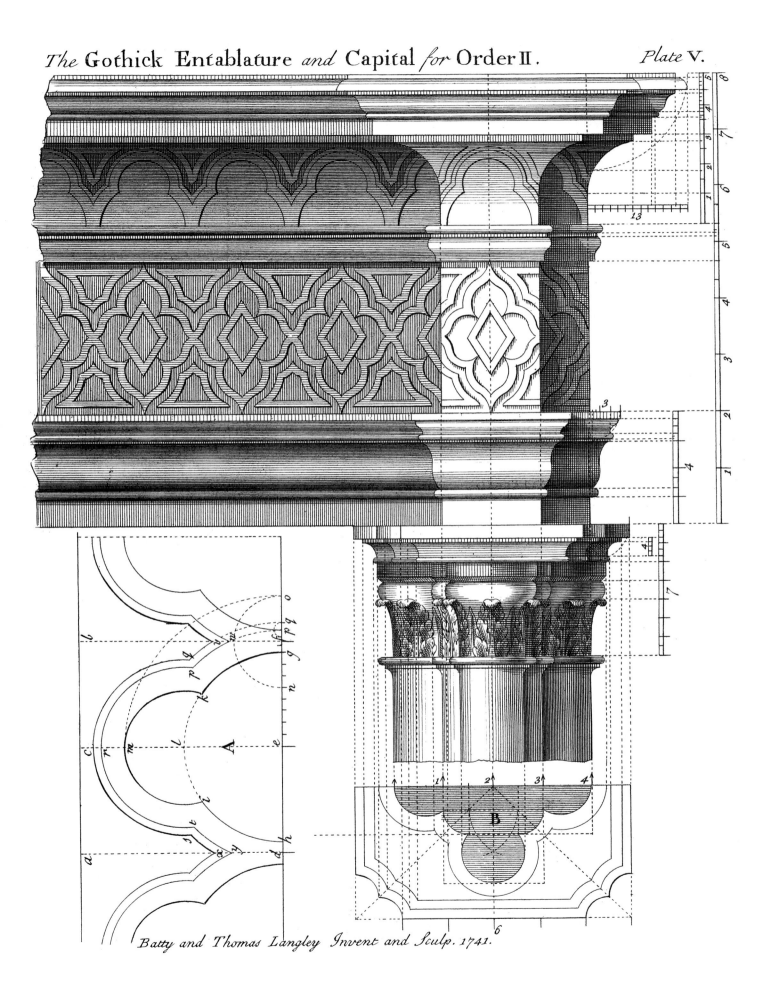

Batty and Thomas Langley Invent and Sculp. 1741.

Batty and Thomas Langley Invent and Sculp. 1741.

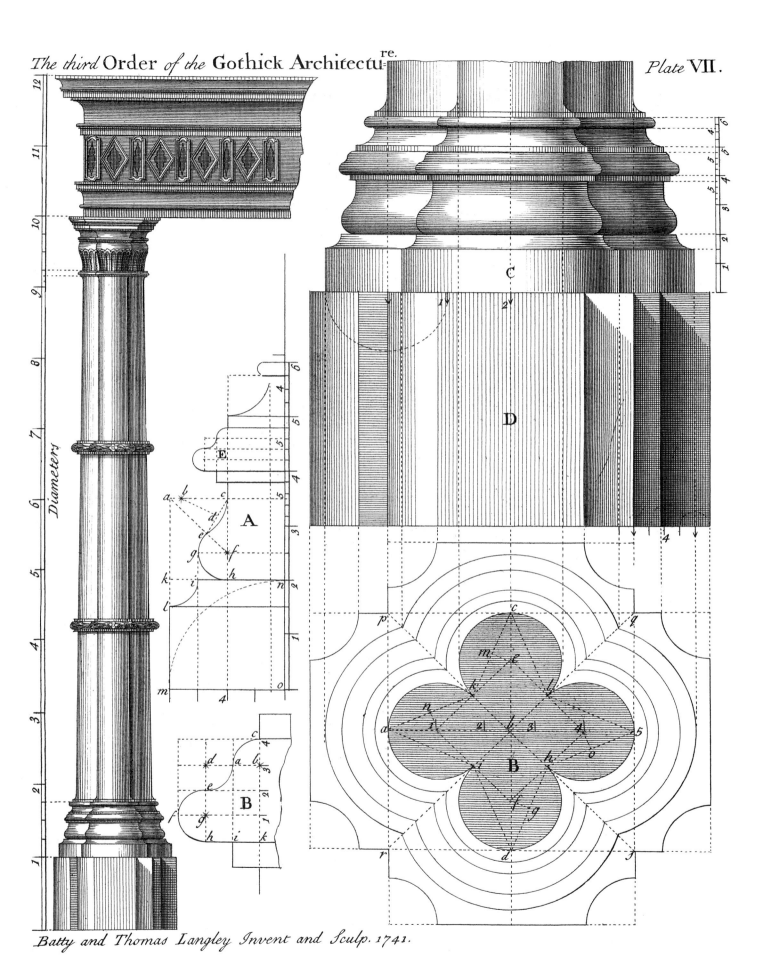

Batty and Thomas Langley Invent and Sculp. 1741.

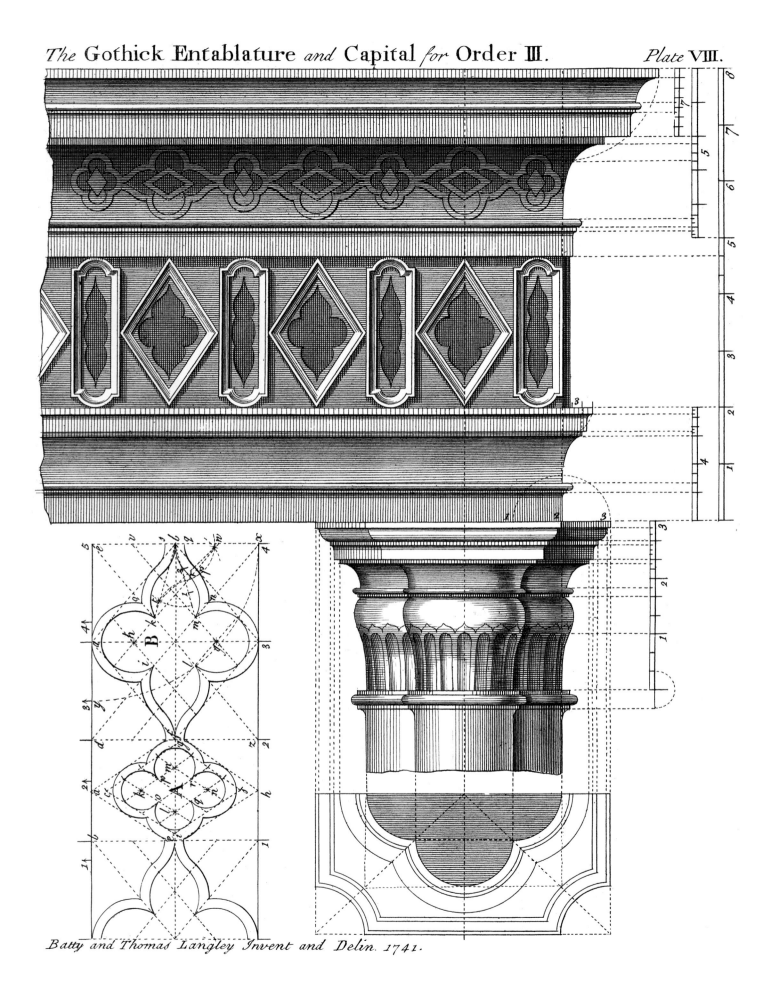

Batty and Thomas Langley Invent and Delin. 1741.

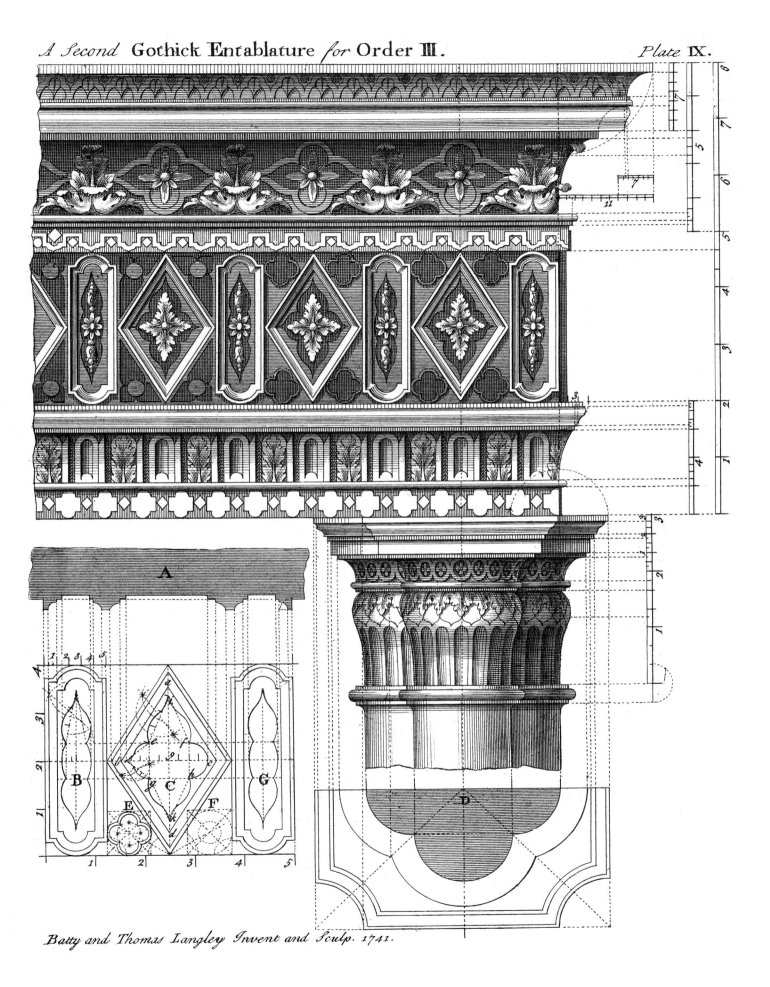

Batty and Thomas Langley Invent and Sculp. 1741.

The Fourth Order of the Gothick Architecture.

Plate X.

Diameters.

A

B

C

D

Batty and Thomas Langley Invent and Sculp. 1741.

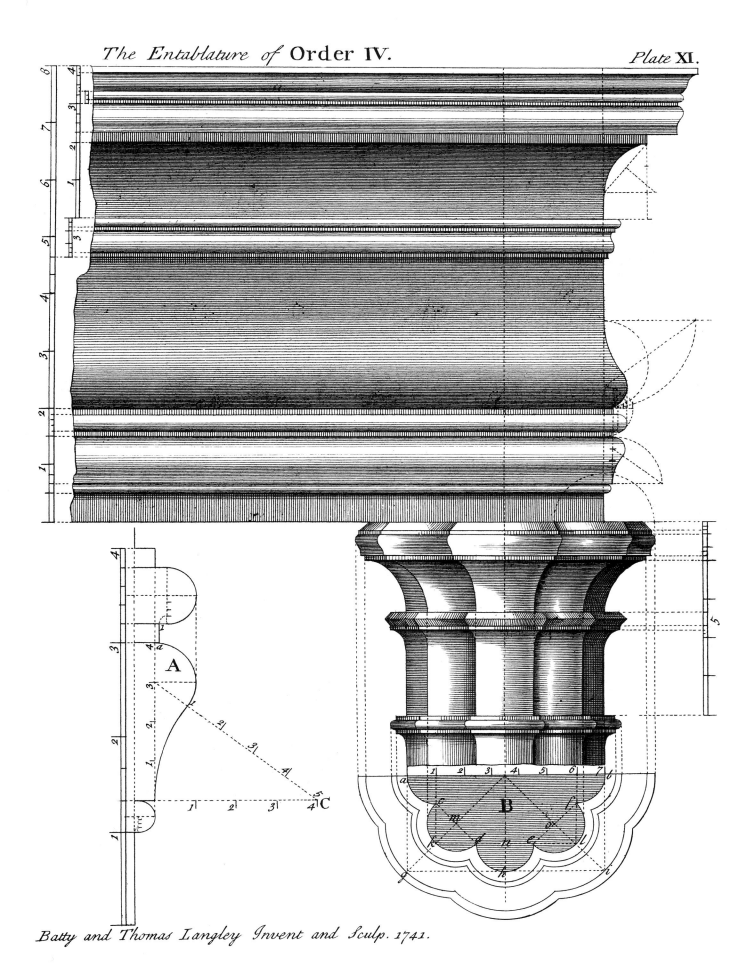

Batty and Thomas Langley Invent and Sculp. 1741.

Batty and Thomas Langley Invent and Sculp. 1741.

The *Fifth* Order *of the* Gothick Architecture.

Plate XIII.

Batty and Thomas Langley Inv. and Sculp. 1741.

Batty and Thomas Langley Inv. and Sculp. 1741.

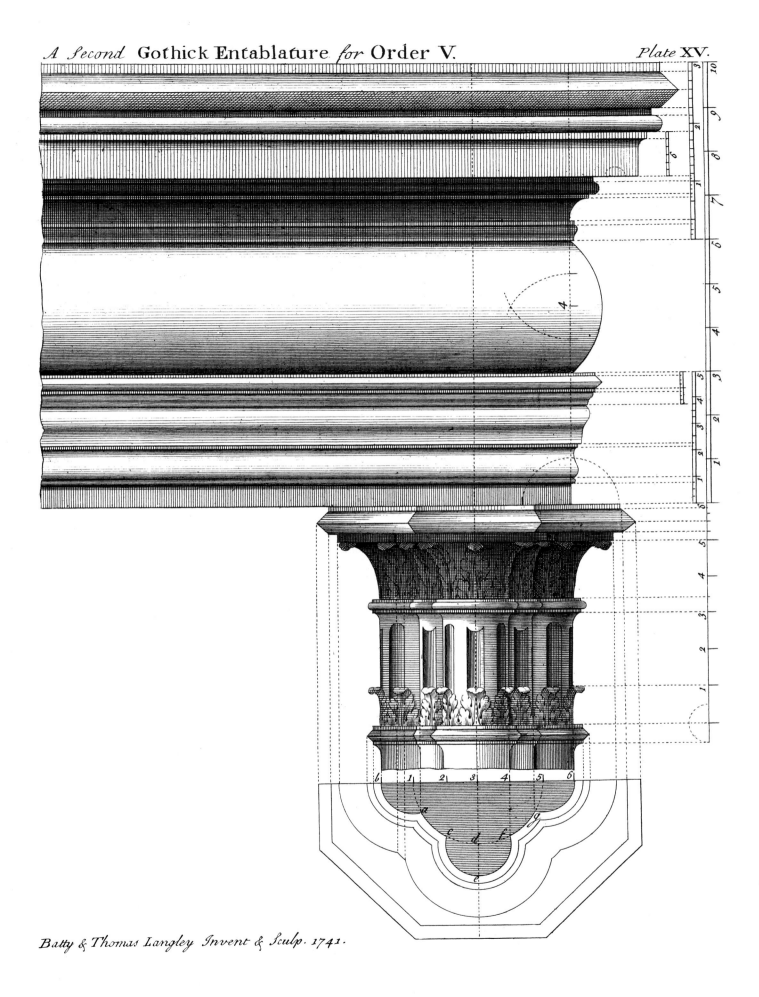

Batty & Thomas Langley Invent & Sculp. 1741.

A *Third* Gothick Entablature *for* Order V.

Plate XVI.

vide A.

vide B

B

A

C

11 parts

Batty & Thomas Langley Inv. & Sculp. 1741.

First **Gothick Frontispiece.**

Plate XVII.

Batty and Thomas Langley *Invent and Sculp.* 1741.

Second **Gothick** Frontispiece.

Plate XVIII.

Batty and Thomas Langley Invent and Sculp. 1741.

Batty and Thomas Langley Inv. and Sculp. 1741.

Fourth Gothick Frontispiece.

Plate **XX**.

Batty and Thomas Langley Inv. and Sculp. 1741.

Fifth Frontispiece.

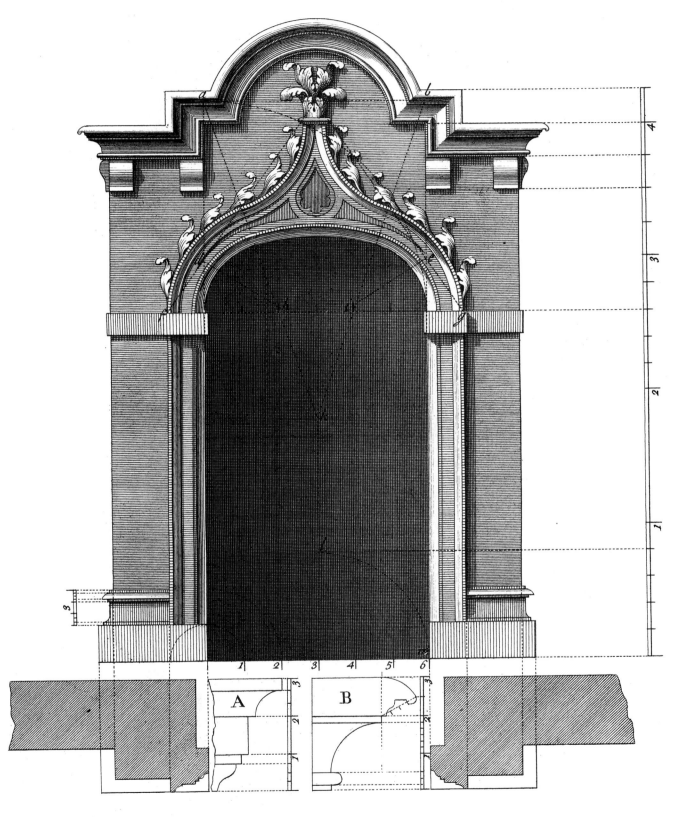

Batty and Tho.ʳ Langley Invent and Sculp. 1741.

Sixth Frontispiece. Plate XXII.

Batty and Tho.ʳ Langley Invent and Sculp. 1741.

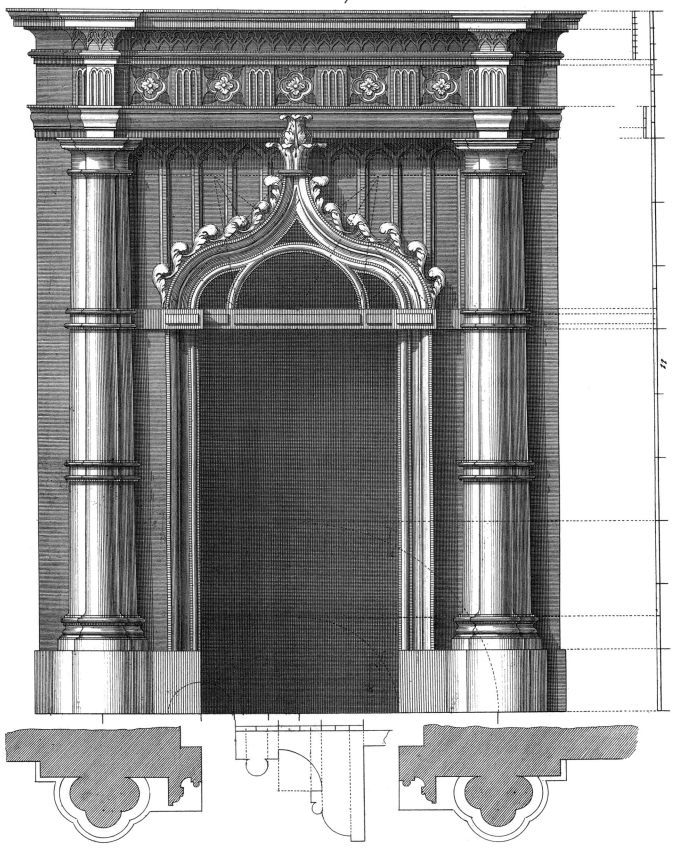

Batty & Tho.ˢ Langley Inv.ᵗ & Sculp 1741

Batty & Tho: Langley Invᵗ & Sculp 1741

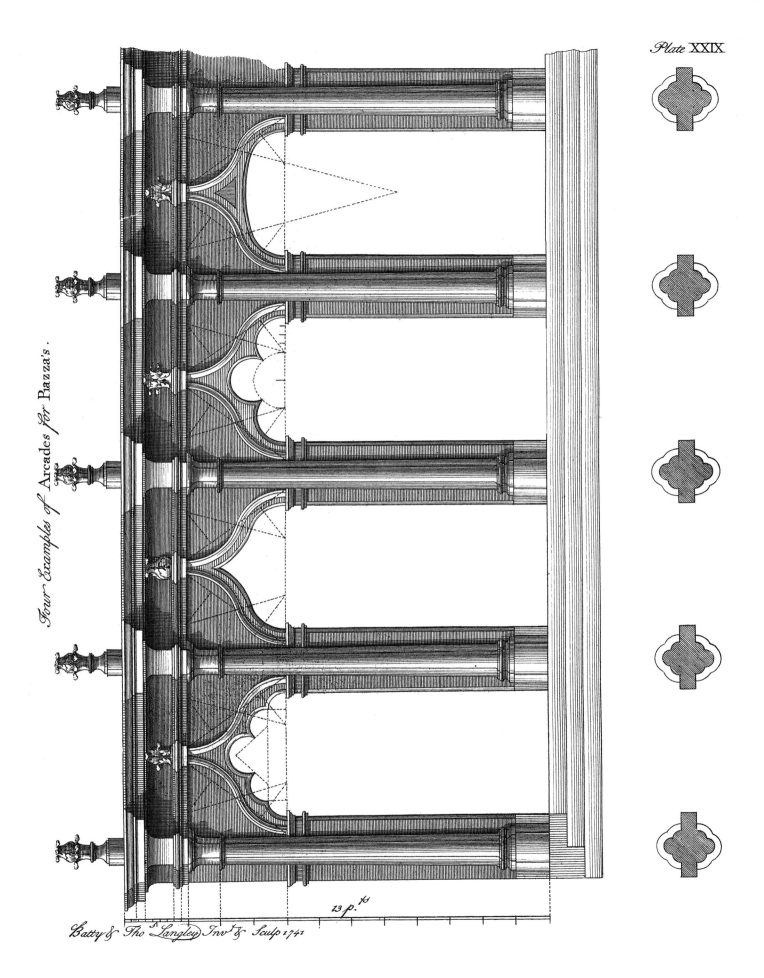

Four Examples of Arcades for Piazza's.

Plate XXIX

Batty & Tho.^S Langley Inv.^t & Sculp 1741

13 p.

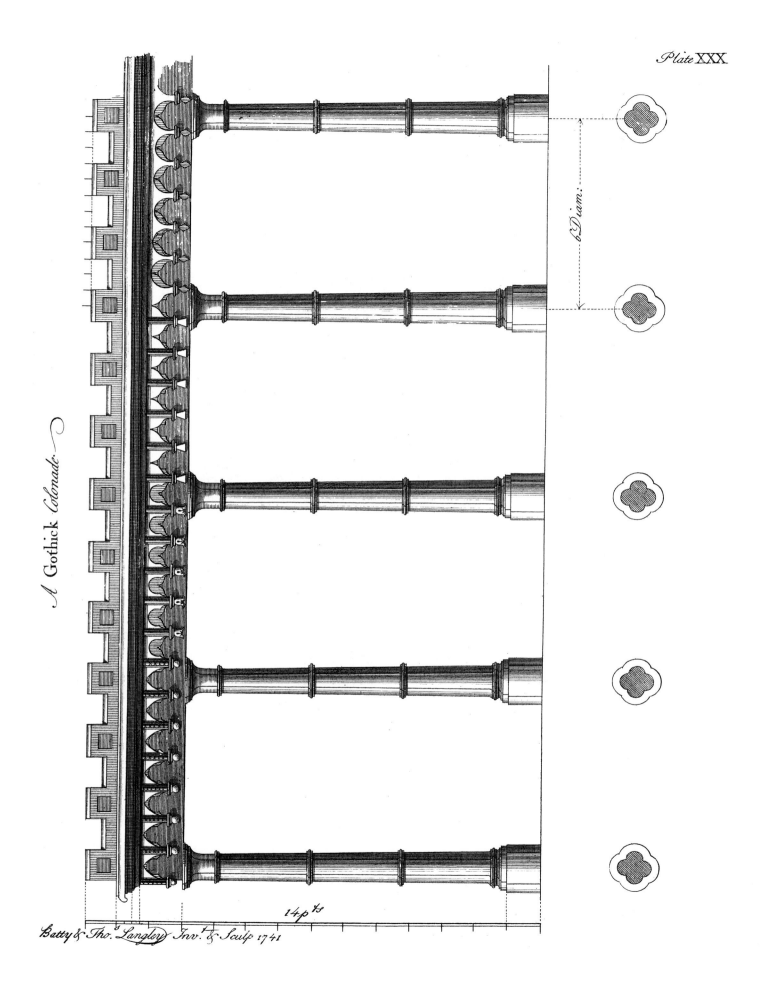

Plate XXX.

A Gothick Colonade.

6 Diam:

14pts

Batty & Thoˢ. Langley Invt. & Sculp 1741

An Umbrello, to a Seat, for to Ter___minate a walk, View, &c in a Garden.

Plate XXXI.

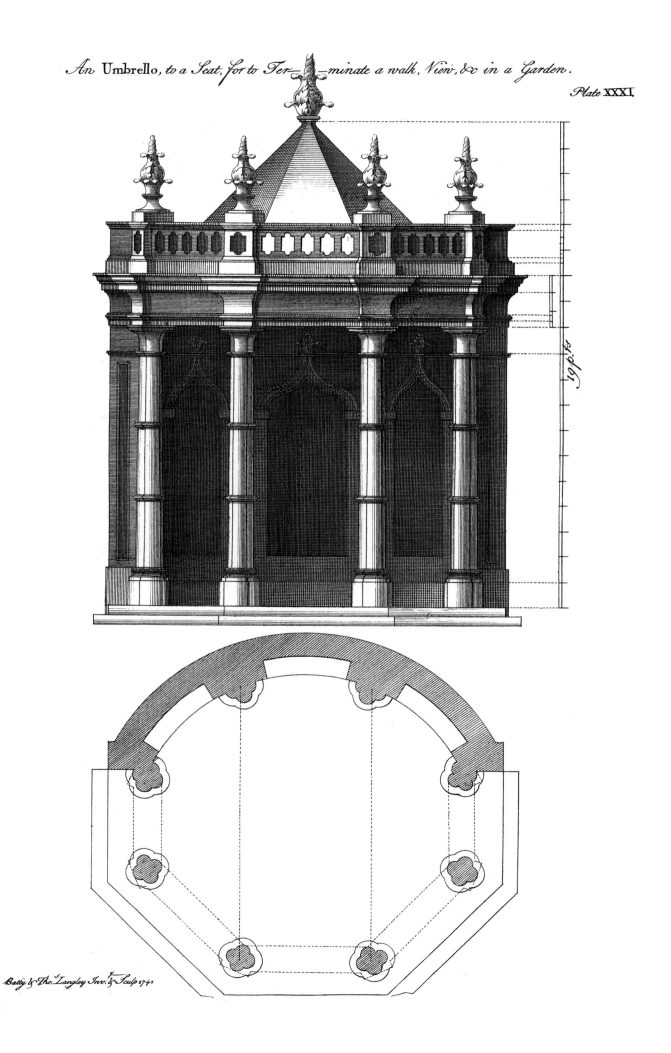

Batty & Tho. Langley Inv. & Sculp 1741.

Gothick   Portico

Plate XXXII

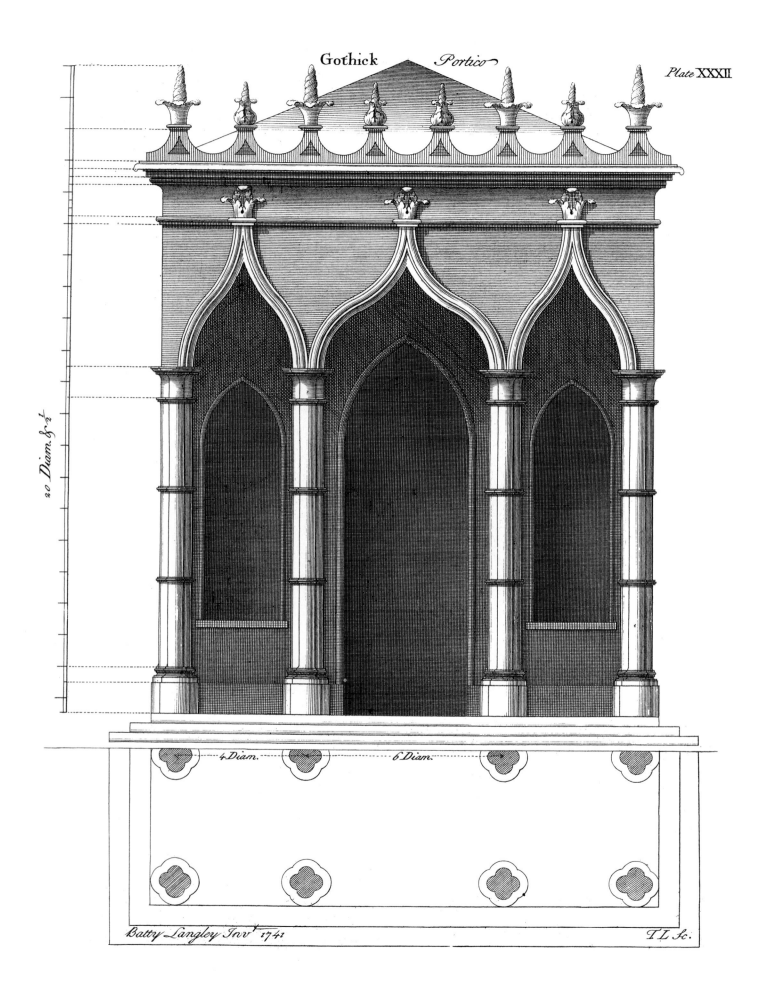

20 Diam. & ½

4 Diam.   6 Diam.

Batty Langley Invᵗ 1741   T L Sc.

Batty & Tho. Langley Inv.t & Sculp 1741

Batty & Tho.ˢ Langley Inv.ᵗ & Sculp 1742

Gothick   *Window*   *Plate* **XXXV**

19 p.ds

Batty Langley Inv.
1742   *TL Sc*

Gothick   Window   Plate **XXXVI**

Batty Langley Invt 1742.   TL Sc.

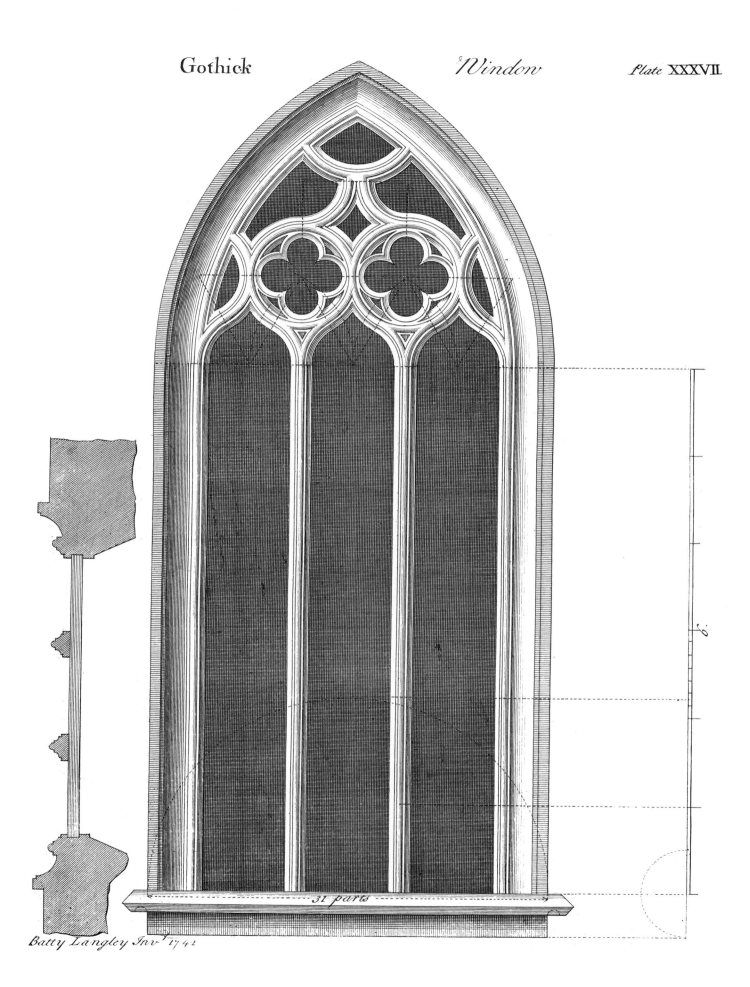

31 parts

Batty Langley Inv.ᵗ 1742

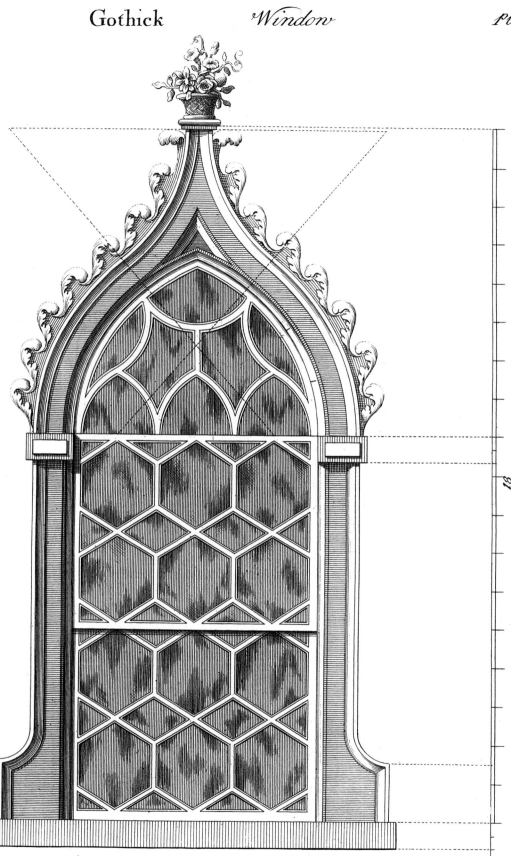

Batty Langley Inv.ᵗ 1742

Gothick *Window* Plate XXXIX

Batty Langley Invt. 1742

Gothick Window for a *Pavillion &c*   Plate XL

Batty Langley Inv. 1742

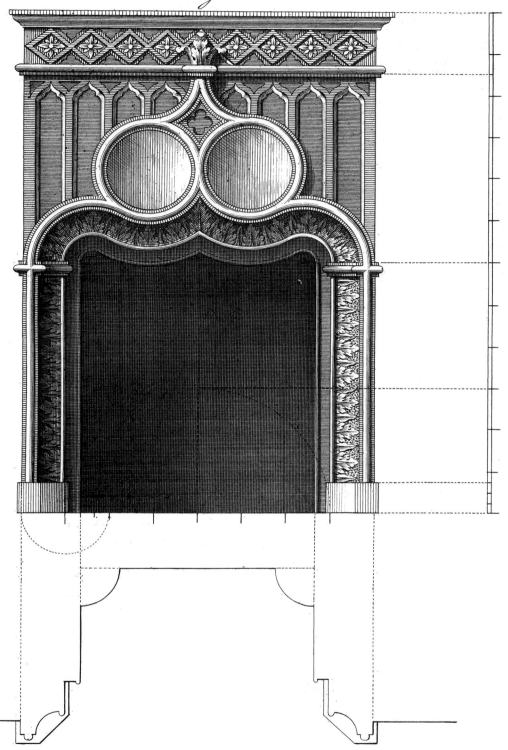

Batty Langley Inv.t 1742 *T. Langley Sc*

Chimney Piece

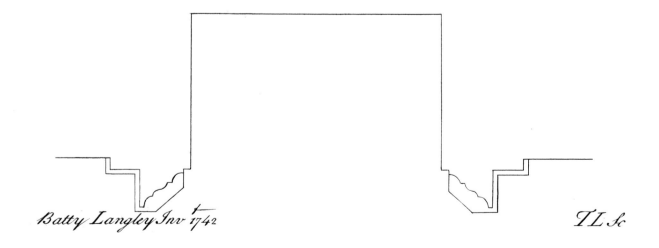

Batty Langley Invt 1742

TL Sc

Plate **XLII**

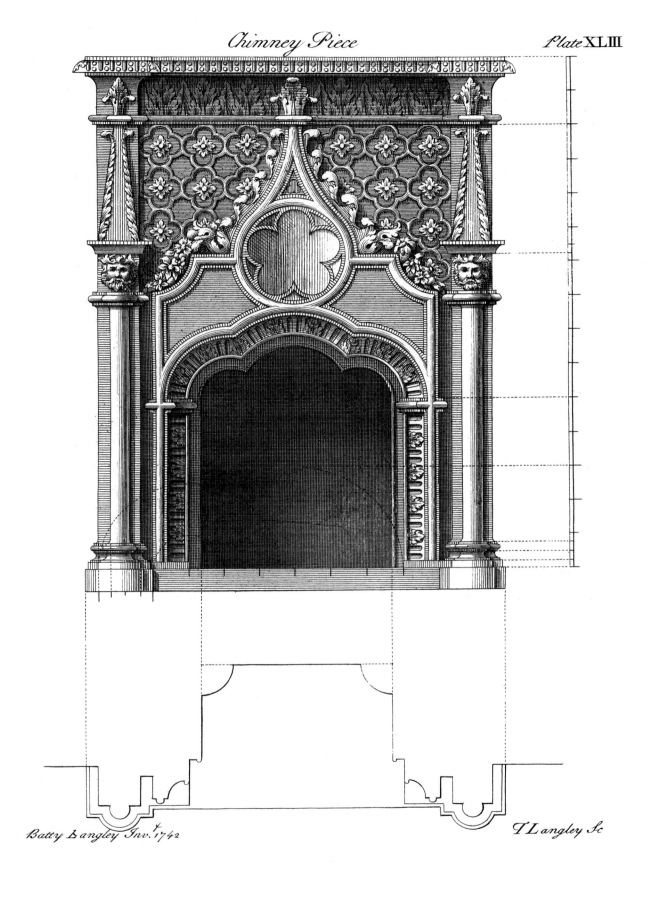

Chimney Piece

Plate XLIII

Batty Langley Invᵗ 1742

T Langley Sc

Batty Langley Inv.t 1742

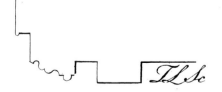

T L Sc

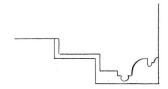

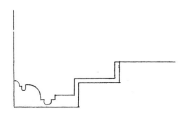

Batty Langley Inv.ᵗ 1742   *TL Sculp*

Plate XLVI

Chimney Piece

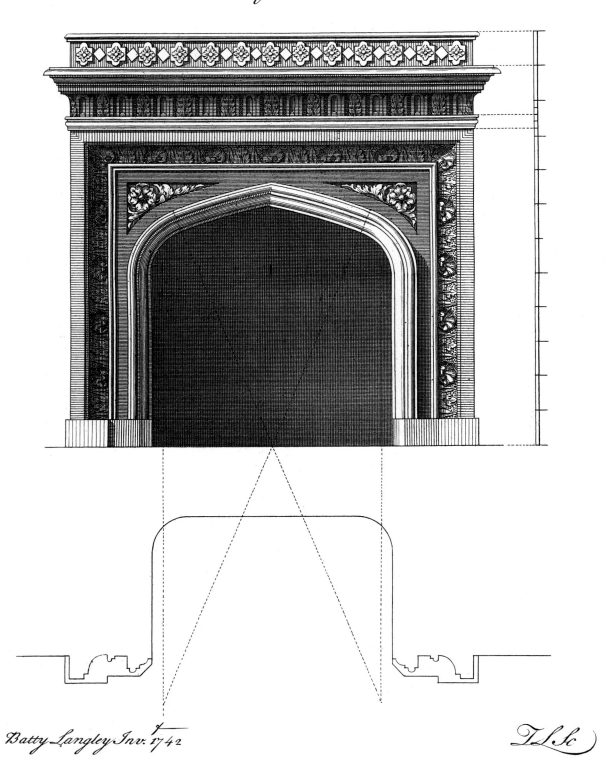

Batty Langley Inv.t 1742

T L Sc

Plate XLVII

Batty Langley Inv. 1742

T L Sc

Plate **XLVIII**

Batty Langley Invt 1742

T L Sc

An Umbrello   Plate XLIX

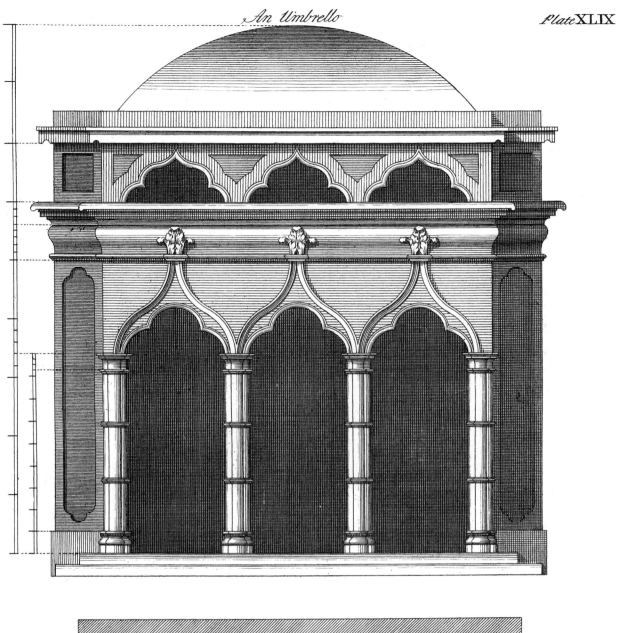

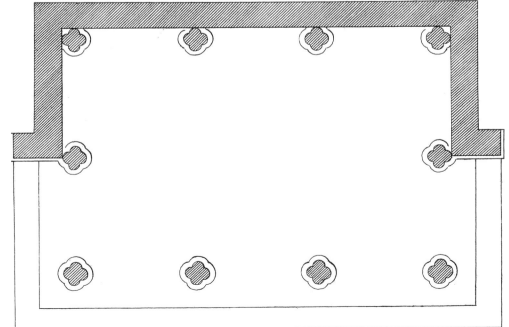

Batty Langley Inv.t 1742   TL Sculp

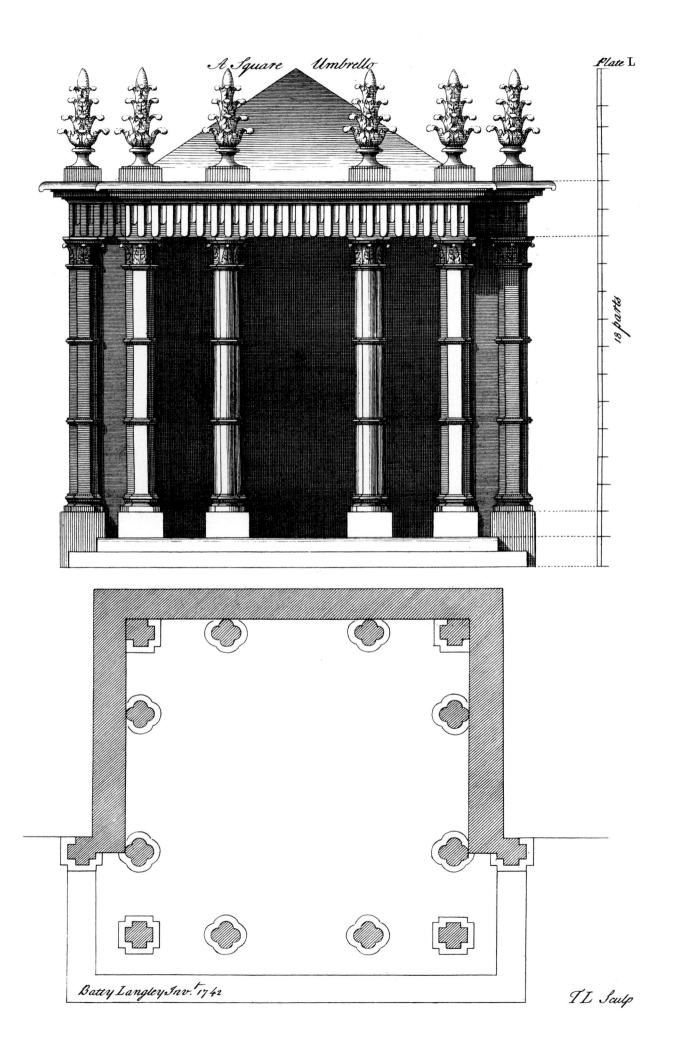

Plate L

A Square Umbrello

18 parts

Batty Langley Invt. 1742

TL Sculp

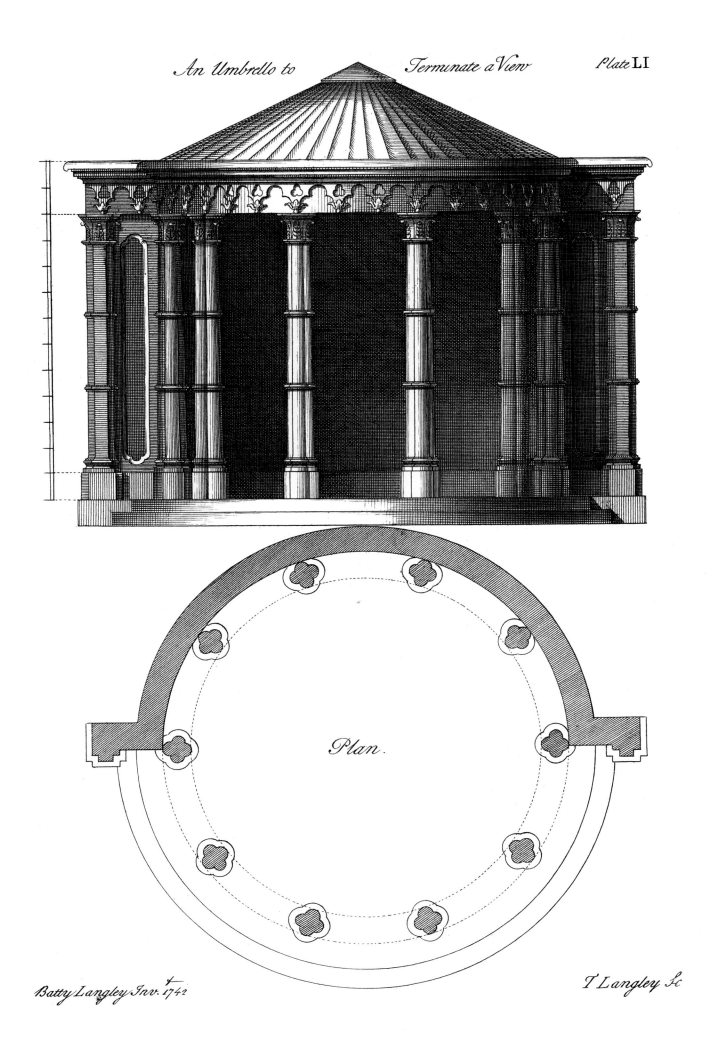

Plan.

Batty Langley Invt 1742　　　　　　　T Langley Sc

Batty Langley Invt. 1742   T L Sc

An Umbrello for the Centre, or Interfection of   Walks in Woods, Wilderneſs's &c Plate LIII

2 Diam

5 Diam

Batty Langley Invt 1742   TL Sculp

An Umbrello for the Centre, or Intersection of Walks, in Woods, Wilderness's &c *Plate* LIV

Batty Langley Invt 1741   TL Sculp

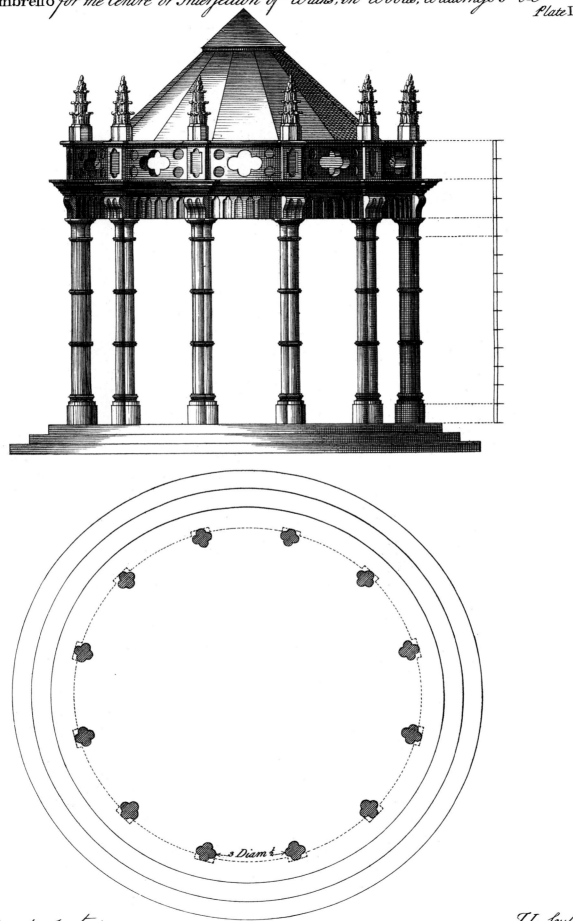

An Umbrello *for the Centre or Interfection of Walks, in Woods, Wilderness's &c*
Plate LV

3 Diam.

Batty Langley Invt 1742

T.L. Sculp

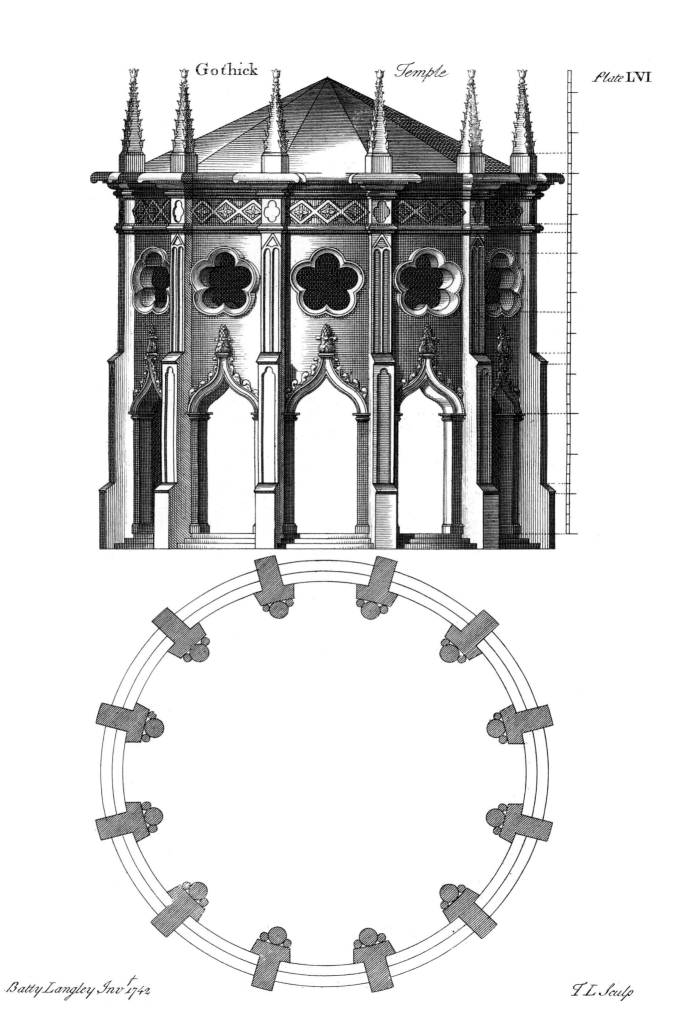

Gothick   Temple   Plate LVI

Batty Langley Inv.t 1742   *T.L. Sculp*

Gothick *Temple*

Plate LVII

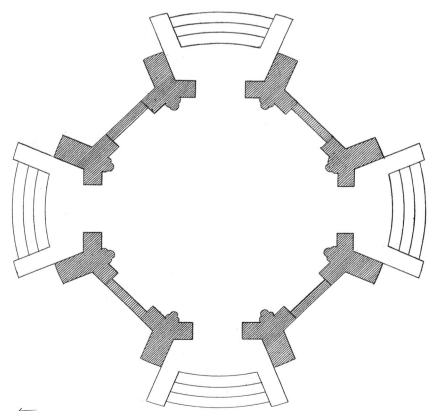

Batty Langley Inv.ᵗ 1742

T. Langley Sculp

Gothick *Temple*

Plate **LVIII**

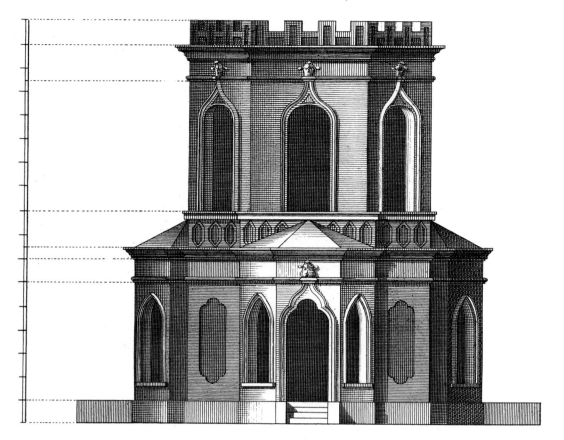

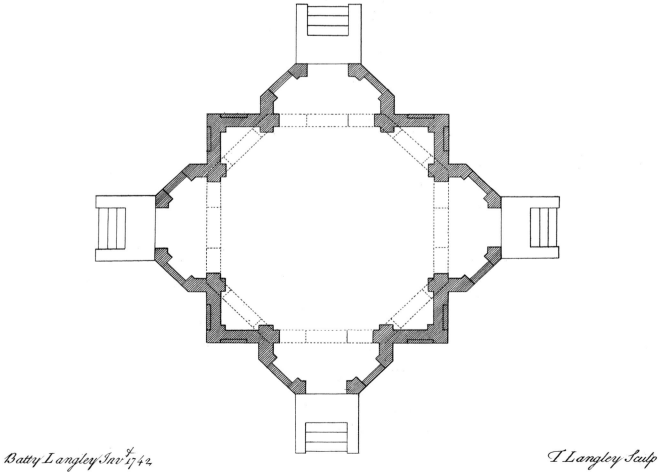

Batty Langley Inv.ᵗ 1742

T. Langley Sculp

Gothick Temple

Plate LIX

Batty Langley Inv.t 1742

T L Sculp

Gothick *Pavillion*

Plate LX

Batty Langley Inv.t 1742

T.L. Sculp.

Plate LXI

Gothick *Pavillion*

Batty Langley Invt 1742

T L Sc

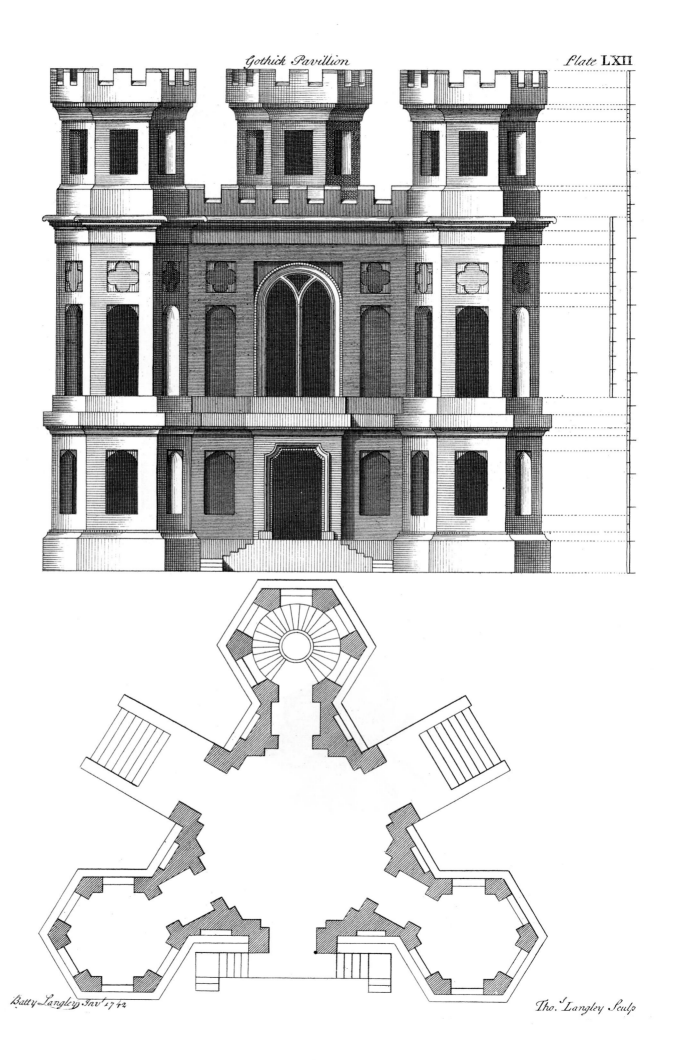

Batty Langley Inv. 1742

Tho.ˢ Langley Sculp

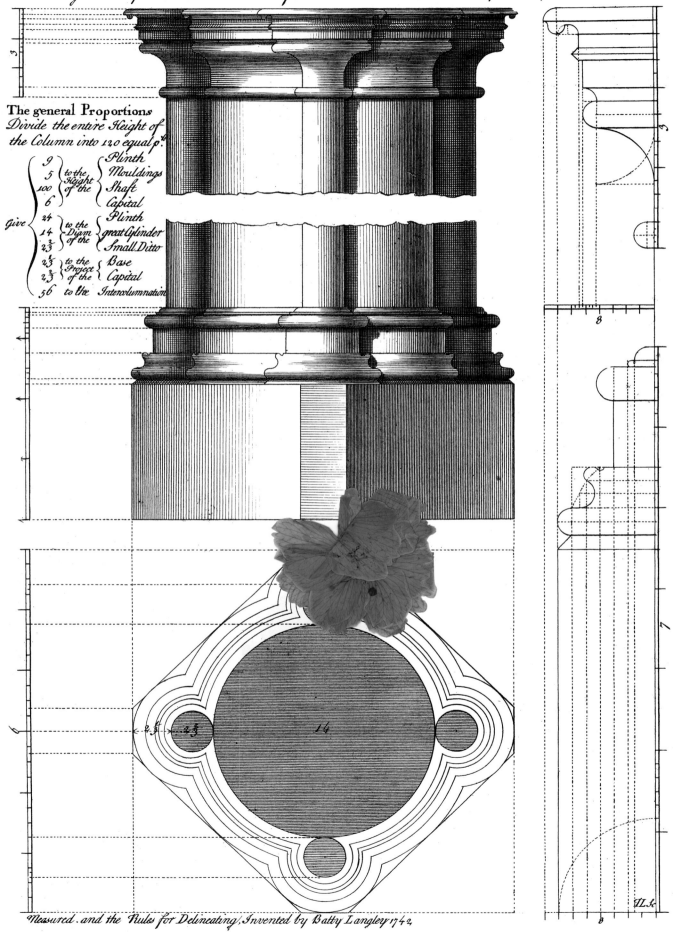

The general Proportions
Divide the entire Height of
the Column into 140 equal p.^{ts}

9	to the Height of the	Plinth
5		Mouldings
100		Shaft
6		Capital
Give 24	to the Diam of the	Plinth
14		great Cylinder
2¾		Small. Ditto
2⅛	to the Project of the	Base
2¾		Capital
56	to the	Intercolumnation

Measured, and the Rules for Delineating, Invented by Batty Langley 1742.

I.L. Sc.

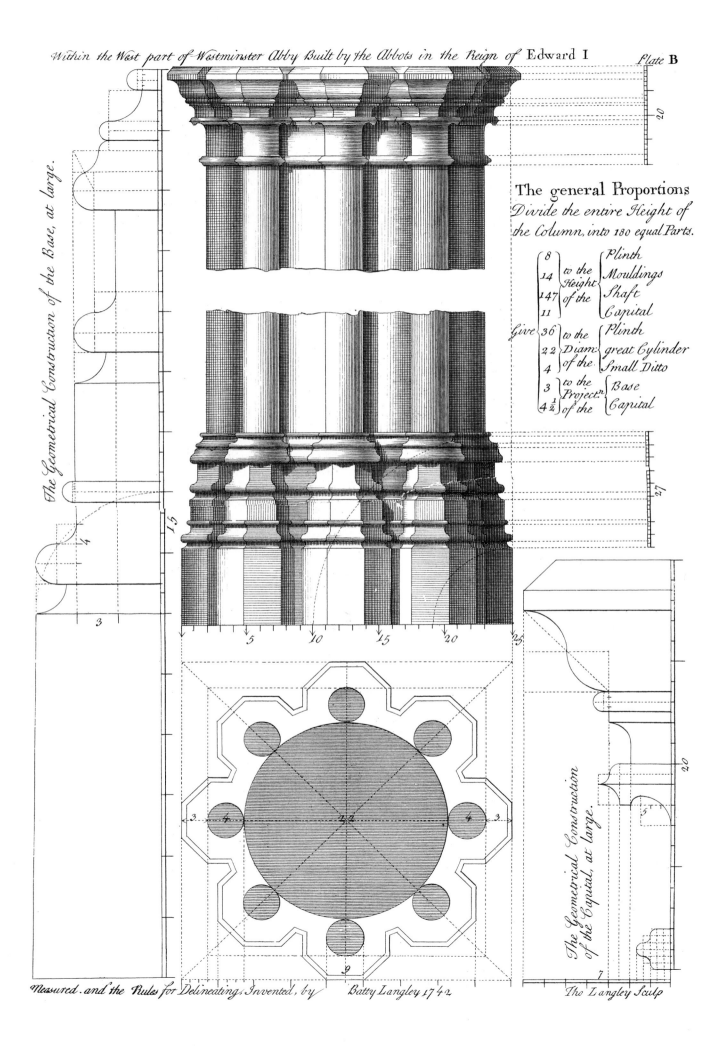

Within the West part of Westminster Abby Built by the Abbots in the Reign of Edward I

Plate **B**

20

The Geometrical Construction of the Base, at large.

The general Proportions

Divide the entire Height of the Column, into 180 equal Parts.

$$\left.\begin{cases} 8 \\ 14 \\ 147 \\ 11 \end{cases}\right\} \text{to the} \\ \text{Height} \\ \text{of the} \left\{\begin{array}{l} Plinth \\ Mouldings \\ Shaft \\ Capital \end{array}\right.$$

Give $\left.\begin{cases} 36 \\ 22 \\ 4 \end{cases}\right\}$ to the Diam: of the $\left\{\begin{array}{l} Plinth \\ great\ Cylinder \\ Small\ Ditto \end{array}\right.$

$\left.\begin{cases} 3 \\ 4\frac{1}{2} \end{cases}\right\}$ to the Projectⁿ of the $\left\{\begin{array}{l} Base \\ Capital \end{array}\right.$

15

4

3

5   10   15   20   25

27

3   4   22   4   3

9

The Geometrical Construction of the Capital, at large.

20

5

7

Measured and the Rules for Delineating Invented, by   Batty Langley 1742

Tho. Langley Sculp

Official
National Test Papers

Maths
Tests

London: The Stationery Office

First published 1998
Second impression 1999

ISBN 0 11 370064 4

Published by The Stationery Office and available from:

The Publications Centre
(mail, telephone and fax orders only)
PO Box 276, London SW8 5DT
General enquiries 0171 873 0011
Telephone orders 0171 873 9090
Fax orders 0171 873 8200

The Stationery Office Bookshops
123 Kingsway, London WC2B 6PQ
0171 242 6393 Fax 0171 242 6394
68-69 Bull Street, Birmingham B4 6AD
0121 236 9696 Fax 0121 236 9699
33 Wine Street, Bristol BS1 2BQ
0117 926 4306 Fax 0117 929 4515
9-21 Princess Street, Manchester M60 8AS
0161 834 7201 Fax 0161 833 0634
16 Arthur Street, Belfast BT1 4GD
01232 238451 Fax 01232 235401
The Stationery Office Oriel Bookshop
The Friary, Cardiff CF1 4AA
01222 395548 Fax 01222 384347
71 Lothian Road, Edinburgh EH3 9AZ
0131 228 4181 Fax 0131 622 7017

The Stationery Office's Accredited Agents
(see Yellow Pages)

and through good booksellers

Key Stage Tests

Mathematics, Key Stage 3, Age 13–14

Contents

Introduction

This is one of three books which will help you work with your child to prepare for the tests almost all children take in Year 9 at the end of Key Stage 3 at about age 14. Using them will also give you some information about what your child knows in English, mathematics and science – known as the core subjects of the National Curriculum.

This book helps you and your child practise the mathematics tests. The other two books help practise the English tests and the science tests.

There are a number of books in the shops which set out to do this. Why are these books the best?

- First, these are the only ones to contain last year's actual tests. When you and your child work through each book, you will be using the actual test questions from last year. In 1999 the test questions will be different but the general appearance of the tests will be much the same.

- Second, you can be sure that the help and advice which surrounds the tests is as helpful as possible. It has been written in liaison with the Qualifications and Curriculum Authority, the official body which produces the tests and advises the Government on the National Curriculum.

The three books contain last year's tests which were taken by 14-year-olds. Using them gives your child a chance to get used to the tests and how to take them. They will also tell you more about how your child is doing in three key subjects, So they are one of the best ways you can help your child make progress.

The tests and how they help your child

Finding out what children know and can do is an important part of their education. It:

■ helps teachers produce better plans and better classroom teaching;

■ helps children think about their own learning;

■ gives you information about your child;

■ helps you help your child at home;

■ builds up a picture of how well schools are doing.

This information is gained in three main ways.

1 Day by day, month by month, term by term, your child's teachers build up a picture of your child through the work they mark and through watching your child at work in the classroom.

 When you get your child's report each year and see your child's teacher in school at an open evening, you will receive a summary of this information.

2 At the ages of 7, 11 and 14 your child's work is assessed more formally. Your child's teachers will use the records they have made and make judgements about how your child is doing against the National Curriculum; this is called Teacher Assessment.

3 At the same time your child will also take the national tests in English, mathematics and science – except for the 7-year-olds, who do not have a science test. Almost every child in the country in those age groups take the same tests. Although they do not test everything, they cover some of the most important work your child has done in school in each of the three subjects.

 When the tests have been marked, your child will be awarded a 'level' in each subject, based on how they performed in the tests. Both the Teacher Assessment levels and the test levels have to be given to you as part of the school's report.

by John O'Leary, Education Editor of *The Times*.

Tests at the end of Key Stage 3 give parents and pupils their last chance to gauge progress before the onset of GCSE. They can be an invaluable guide to areas of strength and weakness, as well as providing an opportunity to polish up that all-important exam technique.

Although the results will not be used for league tables, they do give parents a check on a school's standards at a stage of education which inspectors have often found weak. Schools are obliged not only to publish national curriculum test results, but to set them in a national context.

As the last national tests before GCSE, the Key Stage 3 tests give 14-year-olds the chance to try out their revision skills in an arena which will not affect their long-term prospects. This book allows them to focus their work on the right areas and to plan for the type of questions they will face in the spring.

Assessment now takes place in all national curriculum subjects, but formal tests are limited to the core subjects of English, maths and science. The sample questions in this book are all taken from last year's tests, which will be similar this time.

Schools will run their own revision classes, but a little extra familiarisation, using the test examples, will aid this process. It will also show parents, for whom the tests will be unchartered territory, some of the concepts their children should have mastered by the age of 14.

There is no right or wrong way to prepare for these or any other tests. What suits one child may be quite wrong for another. But there are some basic points that hold good for most examinees, whatever the subject.

Thinking ahead

Perhaps the most important rule, whatever the subject, is not to leave revision to the last moment. Decide what you need to go over several weeks before the test, discuss it with your teacher and set aside some time. Find out what the school's revision plans are, and make sure that your's do not clash.

Do not revise in front of the television. A short period of concentrated work is worth hours shared with *Neighbours* or *Top of the Pops*. Find somewhere quiet, if possible, and do not allow yourself to be distracted.

Use the test examples to get an idea of what will be required in the test, but do not assume that your questions will be in the same areas. Make sure you are confident about all the main topics that you have covered.

In the week of the test

Divide your time between the different subjects, concentrating on weaknesses. Use the practice questions in this book, but do not overdo last-minute revision: you want to be alert for the test itself.

On the day

Make sure you have any materials needed for the test and that you are on time. Then try to relax. In the end, the tests are just another step on the way to GCSE.

What is being tested?

This book contains last years's tests in mathematics for 14-year-olds. These tests are based on the National Curriculum, so you need to know a little about how it's organised.

The National Curriculum for mathematics is divided into five sections (or Attainment Targets):

1. Using and Applying Mathematics;
2. Number;
3. Algebra;
4. Shape, Space and Measures;
5. Handling Data.

The tests

In 1998 the mathematics tests consisted of two written papers, Paper 1 and Paper 2, and a mental arithmetic test. Each written paper took 1 hour and the mental arithmetic test took the form of one taped test consisting of 30 questions and lasting 20 minutes.

Every child takes Paper 1 and Paper 2 at one of four Tiers – Tier 3–5, 4–6, 5–7 or 6–8 – and one or two mental arithmetic tests – Test C (Levels 3–5) or Tests A and B (Levels 4–7) – depending on their level of attainment. Particularly able pupils can also take a written Extension Paper, but that is not included here. In Paper 1 at each of the Tiers and the mental arithmetic test your child will *not* be allowed to use a calculator, but they will be able to do so in Paper 2.

A number of questions in the two papers are duplicated in each Tier (which overlap in levels). Additionally, it is not possible for parents to know beforehand their child's level of attainment and so practise the correct Tier tests. For these reasons, therefore, the questions included in this book are not graded into the four 'Tiers', but are included in order of increasing difficulty, extending from attainment Level 3 to Level 8. This enables you to work with your child to practise the tests to a level at which they are comfortable. Don't expect your child to answer all the questions. The Extension Paper is not included.

Transcripts of the mental arithmetic Tests A, B and C are included for you to do with your child, and answer sheets are provided for his or her answers. As with the written test papers, it is not possible for you to know beforehand whether your child should do the lower Tier Test C or higher Tier Tests A and B, but you can practice the tests with your child to the level at which they are comfortable.

How you can help your child prepare for the mathematics tests

- Be encouraging and supportive, so that your child is confident about the tests.

- Talk with your child's teacher about how you can help your child improve, so that you can support and build on the work done in class.

- Be interested in your child's work and talk about it. Try not to nag or be critical.

- Try to take advantage of opportunities to get your child to do mental arithmetic or to use mathematics in practical everyday situations, such as shopping, comparing and estimating prices, weighing and measuring things, looking at graphs, diagrams, charts, etc, in books, newspapers and magazines, and saying what they mean.

- Don't let your own worries about tests – if you have any – pass on to your child.

Hints for your child on taking the tests

1. Listen carefully to the teacher's instructions for the tests and follow them exactly.

2. Read the questions carefully.

3. If you're not sure, ask for help. The teacher can't tell you the answers but will be able to help you understand what it is you have to do.

4. Don't be afraid to make a sensible guess if you are not entirely sure of the answer.

5. Don't worry if you can't answer all the questions, leave out the ones you can't do and make sure you do answer all the ones you can.

6. If you get stuck on a question, move on to the next one and come back to it later.

7. If there's time after you've tried all the questions, check the answers very carefully.

Guidance on administering the tests

- You should try to maintain appropriate test conditions by ensuring that your child is able to work undisturbed.

- Make sure that your child has the appropriate equipment listed on the front cover of the relevant paper. Note that a calculator **must not** be used for any of Paper 1 or for the mental arithmetic test, but is **required** for some questions in Paper 2.

- Make sure that your child sees the 'Remember' section at the front of the test paper, and the instructions and formulae on pages 2 and 3 of each set of questions.

- Give appropriate time reminders, for example half-way through the test and again 10 minutes before the end.

You should ensure that your child is clear about what he or she has to do. You may answer questions such as 'Am I supposed to write it here?' or 'Do I have to do all the questions?' or clarify the meaning of instructions given in the test papers, but you must not help with the mathematics being tested. If your child asks for clarification of the mathematical symbols or notation used in questions, you should read them to your child, but you should **not** indicate the operation or process involved. For example you may say that '%' means 'per cent' but **not** that it means 'out of a hundred'; or that 'x^2' means 'x squared' but **not** that it means ' x times x'.

Combined Paper 1
Questions, 1998
Levels 3-8

Write your name and school in the spaces below.

First Name _____

Last Name _____

School _____

Remember

- Answer as many questions as you can in 1 hour. You are *not* expected to answer all the questions.

- You **must not** use a calculator for any question in this test.

- You will need: pen, pencil, rubber, ruler, angle measurer or protractor, pair of compasses, tracing paper and mirror (optional).

- Some formulae you might need are on page 3.

- This test starts with easier questions.

- Write all your answers and working on the test paper – do not use any rough paper.

- Check your work carefully.

- Ask if you are not sure what to do.

Instructions

Answers

This means:
show your working and
write down your answer.

Calculators

You **must not** use a calculator to
answer any question in this test.

Formulae

You might need to use these formulae.

AREA

Circle

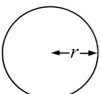

πr^2

Take π as 3.14

Triangle

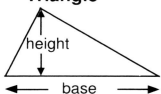

$\dfrac{\text{base} \times \text{height}}{2}$

Parallelogram

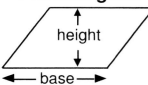

$\text{base} \times \text{height}$

Trapezium

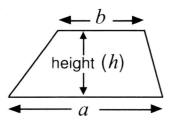

$\dfrac{(a + b)}{2} \times h$

LENGTH

Circle

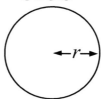

$\text{circumference} = 2\pi r$

For a right-angled triangle

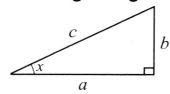

$a^2 + b^2 = c^2$ (Pythagoras' theorem)

$a = c \cos x \qquad \cos x = \dfrac{a}{c}$

$b = c \sin x \qquad \sin x = \dfrac{b}{c}$

$b = a \tan x \qquad \tan x = \dfrac{b}{a}$

VOLUME

Prism

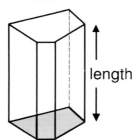

area of cross-section × length

1.

Look at this bus timetable, from Highbury to Colton:

Bus Timetable: Highbury to Colton					
Highbury *depart:*	07:45	08:30	09:30	10:45	11:30
Colton *arrive:*	08:30	09:15	10:15	11:30	12:15

(a) A bus leaves **Highbury** at **08:30**
What time does it arrive in **Colton**?

. . . .
1 mark

How much time does the bus journey take ?

.... minutes

. . . .
1 mark

(b) 5 friends are going from Highbury to Colton by bus.
They want to **arrive by 10:30**
Which is the **latest** bus they can catch from Highbury?

. . . .
1 mark

(c) Each bus ticket costs **£2.20**
How much do the **5** bus tickets cost altogether?

£

. . . .
1 mark

2.

(a) **Two** of these angles are the **same size**.
Put rings around the two angles which are the same size.

. . . .
1 mark

(b) Draw an angle which is **bigger** than a **right angle**.

. . . .
1 mark

(c) Kelly is facing **North**.
She turns **clockwise** through **2 right angles**.
Which direction is she facing now?

. . . .

. . . .
1 mark

(d) Aled is facing **West**.
He turns **clockwise** through **3 right angles**.
Which direction is he facing now?

. . . .
1 mark

. . . .

3.

The table shows the distance in miles along the railway line from Shrewsbury to some other stations.

	Miles from Shrewsbury
Shrewsbury	0 miles
Welshpool	20 miles
Newtown	34 miles
Caersws	39 miles
Borth	73 miles
Aberystwyth	82 miles

(a) What is the distance between **Shrewsbury** and **Welshpool**?

. . . .

1 mark

(b) What is the distance between **Welshpool** and **Borth**?

. . . .

1 mark

(c) What is the distance between **Borth** and **Aberystwyth**?

. . . .

1 mark

(c) Find the answers.

524 − 249 =

. . . .
1 mark

46 × 8 =

. . . .
1 mark

144 ÷ 9 =

. . . .
1 mark

7.

(a) A shop sells video tapes for **£2.50** each.

What is the cost of **16** video tapes?

£ . . . .
1 mark

(b) The shop sells audio cassettes.
Each cassette costs **£1.49**

What is the cost of **4** cassettes?

£ . . . .
1 mark

(c) **How many cassettes** can you buy with **£12**?

. . . .
1 mark

(d) The shop also sells cassettes in **packs** of **three**.
A pack costs **£3.99**

How many packs can you buy with **£12**?

. . . .
1 mark

Pack of three: £3.99   **Single cassette: £1.49**

(e)   What is the **greatest number** of cassettes you can buy with **£15**?

You can buy some packs **and** some single cassettes.

. . . .

1 mark

8.

In a magic square, each **row**, **column** and **diagonal** adds up to the same number.

For example, each row, column and diagonal in **this** magic square adds up to **15**

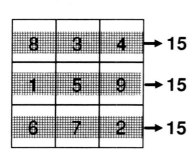 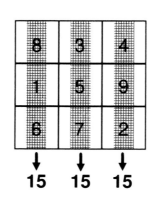 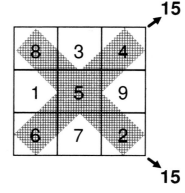

Here is another magic square.

Use the numbers in the first row of this magic square to work out what each row, column and diagonal must add up to.

Then complete the magic square.

24	34	5
2	....	....
37	....	18

24 + 34 + 5 = ...

....
1 mark

....
1 mark

....
1 mark

....
1 mark

Here are the ingredients for **1** fruit cake:

> **1 fruit cake**
> 200g self-raising flour
> 100g caster sugar
> 150g margarine
> 125g mixed fruit
>   3 eggs

(a) Complete the table to show how much of each ingredient you need to make **10** fruit cakes.

Give your answers in grams **and** in kilograms.

> **10 fruit cakes**
>
> ..2000.. g = ...2.... kg self-raising flour
>
> .... g = ... kg caster sugar
>
> .... g = ... kg margarine
>
> .... g = ... kg mixed fruit
>
>   30   eggs

. . . .
1 mark

. . . .

. . . .
2 marks

(b) **6** eggs cost **70p**

How much will **30** eggs cost?

£

. . . .
1 mark

A jigsaw has three different sorts of piece.

Corner pieces,
with **2** straight
sides

Edge pieces,
with **1** straight
side

Middle pieces,
with **0** straight
sides

(a) This jigsaw has **24** pieces
altogether, in **4** rows of **6**.

Complete the table below to
show how many of each sort
of piece this jigsaw has.

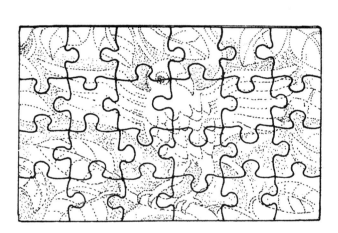

Corner pieces: ....

Edge pieces: ....

Middle pieces: ....

Total: 24

....
1 mark

(b) Another jigsaw has **42** pieces
altogether, in **6** rows of **7**.

Complete the table below to
show how many of each sort
of piece this jigsaw has.

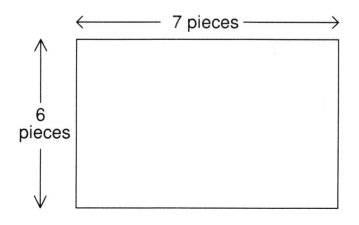

⟵———— 7 pieces ————⟶

6
pieces

Corner pieces: ....

Edge pieces: ....

Middle pieces: ....

Total: 42

....
....
2 marks

(c) A **square** jigsaw has **64 middle** pieces.

Complete the table below to show how many of each sort of piece the **square** jigsaw has, and the total number of pieces.

Remember that the total must be a **square** number.

Corner pieces: ....

Edge pieces: ....

Middle pieces: 64

Total: ....

. . . .

. . . .

2 marks

11.

This is how Caryl works out **15% of 120** in her head.

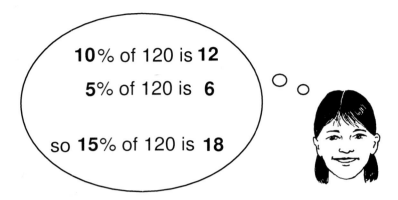

10% of 120 is **12**

5% of 120 is **6**

so **15**% of 120 is **18**

(a) Show how Caryl can work out **17½% of 240** in her head.

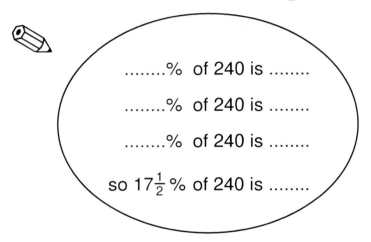

........% of 240 is ....

........% of 240 is ....

........% of 240 is ....

so 17½ % of 240 is ....

. . . .

. . . .

2 marks

(b) Work out **35% of 520**.
Show your working.

. . . .

. . . .

2 marks

18

12.

(a) A teacher needs **220** booklets.
The booklets are in **packs of 16**.

How many packs must the teacher order?

Show your working.

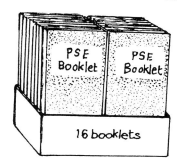

.... packs

. . . .

. . . .
2 marks

(b) Each booklet weighs **48g**.

How much do the **220** booklets weigh **altogether**?
Show your working. Give your answer in **kg**.

.... kg

. . . .

. . . .
2 marks

. . . .
1 mark

13.

(a) Elin has a bag of marbles.

You cannot see how many marbles are inside the bag.

Call the number of marbles which Elin starts with in her bag **n**.

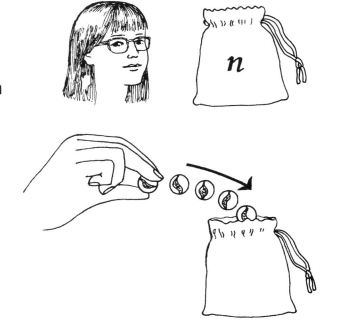

Elin puts **5 more** marbles **into** her bag.

Write an expression to show the total number of marbles in Elin's bag now.

. . . .
1 mark

(b) Ravi has another bag of marbles.

Call the number of marbles which Ravi starts with in his bag **t**.

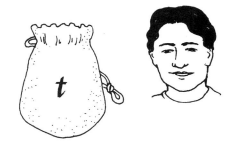

Ravi takes **2** marbles **out** of his bag.

Write an expression to show the total number of marbles in Ravi's bag now.

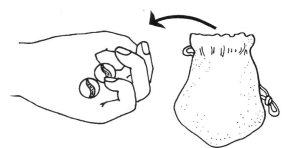

. . . .
1 mark

(c) Jill has **3** bags of marbles.

Each bag has p marbles inside.

Jill takes some marbles out.

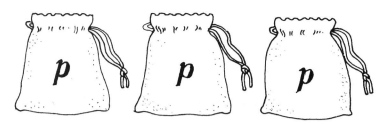

Now the total number of marbles in Jill's 3 bags is $3p - 6$

Some of the statements below **could** be **true**.
Put a tick (✓) by each statement which **could** be **true**.

Jill took **2** marbles out of **one** of the bags, and **none** out of the other bags.	
Jill took **2** marbles out of **each** of the bags.	
Jill took **3** marbles out of **one** of the bags, and **none** out of the other bags.	
Jill took **3** marbles out of each of **two** of the bags, and **none** out of the other bag.	
Jill took **6** marbles out of **one** of the bags, and **none** out of the other bags.	
Jill took **6** marbles out of each of **two** of the bags, and **none** out of the other bag.	

. . . .

. . . .

2 marks

The pupils in five classes did a quiz.

The graphs below show the scores in each class. Each class had a mean score of 7. In three of the classes, 80% of the pupils got more than the mean score.

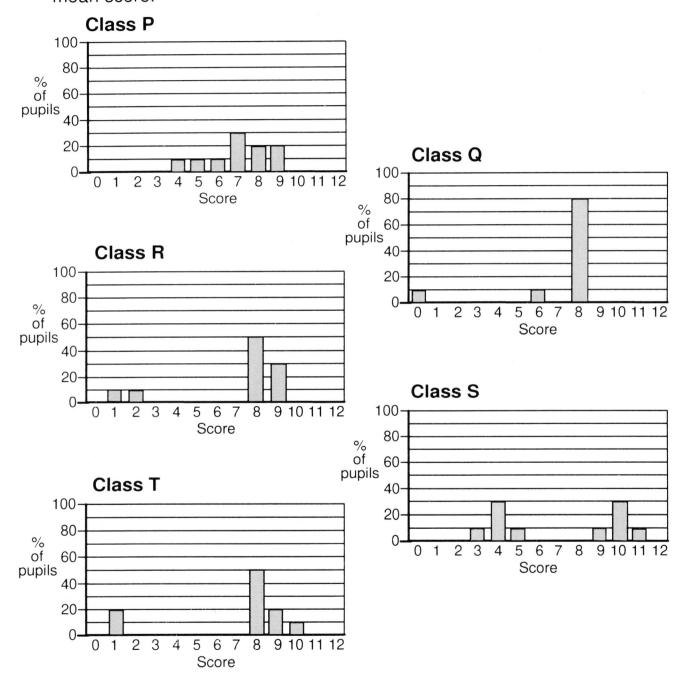

(a) In which **three** classes did **80%** of the pupils score **more than 7**?

....

....

2 marks

Class ....   and   Class........   and   Class ....

(b) Look at the graphs which show that 80% of the pupils scored more than 7.

Some of the statements below are **true** when 80% of the pupils scored more than 7.

Put a tick (✓) by each statement which is **true**.

All of the pupils scored **at least 2**	
Most of the pupils scored **at least 8**	
Most of the pupils scored **at least 10**	
Some of the pupils scored **less than 6**	

. . . .

. . . .

2 marks

(c) In another quiz the **mean score** was **6**.

Complete this graph to show a mean score of 6.

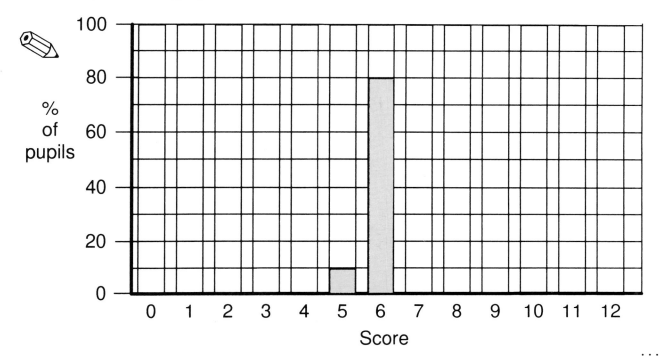

. . . .

1 mark

15.

Here are five containers:

A   B   C   D   E

Water is poured at a constant rate into **three** of the containers.
The graphs show the **depth** of water as the containers fill up.

graph 1   graph 2   graph 3

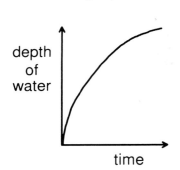 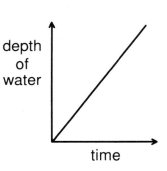 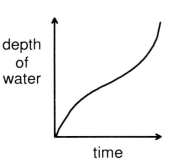

Fill in the gaps below to show which container matches each graph.

Graph 1 matches container ....

. . . .

Graph 2 matches container ....

. . . .

Graph 3 matches container ....

. . . .

3 marks

16.

Look at this diagram:

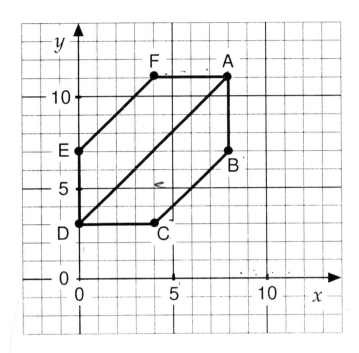

(a) The line through points A and F has the equation $y = 11$

What is the equation of the line through points **A** and **B**?

. . . .

1 mark

(b) The line through points A and D has the equation $y = x + 3$

What is the equation of the line through points **F** and **E**?

. . . .

1 mark

(c) What is the equation of the line through points **B** and **C**?

. . . .

1 mark

17.

Each shape in this question has an **area** of **10cm²**.
No diagram is drawn to scale.

(a) Calculate the height of the parallelogram.

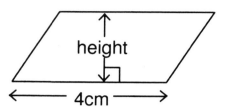

area = 10cm²   height = ... cm

. . . .
1 mark

(b) Calculate the length of the base of the triangle.

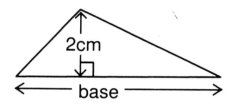

area = 10cm²   base = ... cm

. . . .
1 mark

(c) What might be the values of h, a and b in this trapezium?
(a is greater than b)

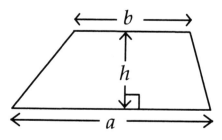

area = 10cm² h = ... cm a = ... cm b = ... cm

. . . .
1 mark

What else might the values of h, a and b be?

area = 10cm² h = ... cm a = ... cm b = ... cm

. . . .
1 mark

(d) Look at this rectangle:

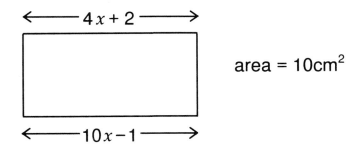

area = 10cm^2

Calculate the value of x and use it to find the length and width of the rectangle.

Show your working.

area = 10cm^2 length = ... cm   width = ... cm

2 marks

18.

This is a series of patterns with grey and white tiles.

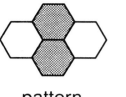

pattern
number
1

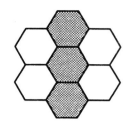

pattern
number
2

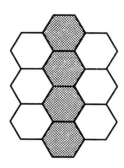

pattern
number
3

The series of patterns continues by adding 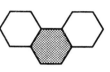 each time.

(a) Complete this table:

pattern number	number of **grey** tiles	number of **white** tiles
5		
16		

. . . .

. . . .

2 marks

(b) Complete this table by writing **expressions**:

pattern number	expression for the number of **grey** tiles	expression for the number of **white** tiles
n		

. . . .

. . . .

2 marks

(c) Write an expression to show the **total** number of tiles in pattern number n.
Simplify your expression.

. . . .

1 mark

(d) A different series of patterns is made with tiles.

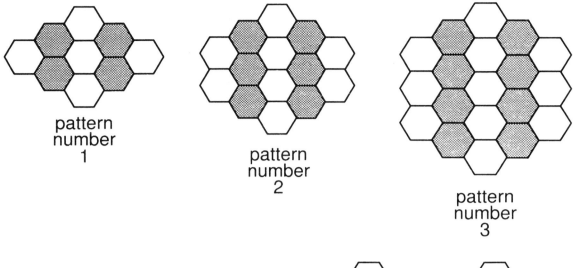

pattern
number
1

pattern
number
2

pattern
number
3

The series of patterns continues by adding  each time.

For this series of patterns, write an expression to show the **total** number of tiles in pattern number n.

Show your working and **simplify** your expression.

. . . .

. . . .

2 marks

Sixty

19.

(a) Each of these calculations has the same answer, **60**

Fill in each gap with a number.

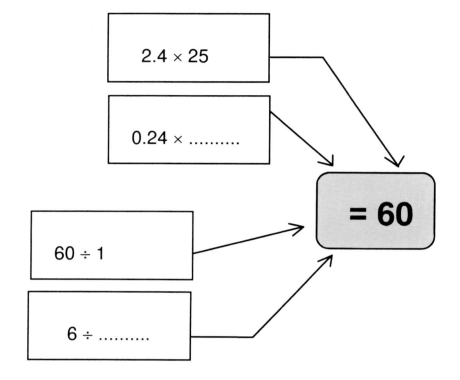

2.4×25

$0.24 \times$ ....

$60 \div 1$

$6 \div$ ....

= 60

....
1 mark

....
1 mark

(b) Solve these equations to find the values of a, b and c.

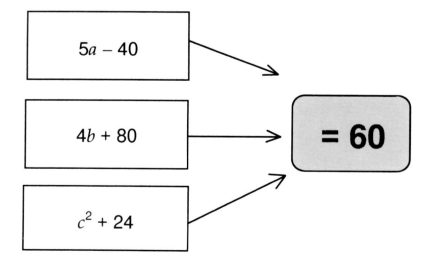

$5a - 40$

$4b + 80$

$c^2 + 24$

= 60

$a =$ .... $b =$ .... $c =$ ....

....
....
....
3 marks

(c) Solve these simultaneous equations to find the values of x and y.

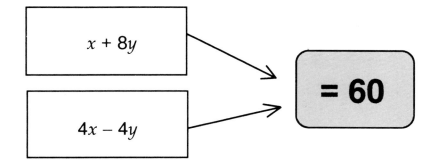

$$x + 8y$$

$$4x - 4y$$

$$= 60$$

Show your working.

· · · ·

· · · ·

· · · ·

3 marks

$x =$ .... $y =$ ....

20.

In the scale drawing, the shaded area represents a lawn.

There is a wire fence **all around** the lawn.
The shortest distance from the fence to the edge of the lawn
is **always 6m**.

On the diagram, draw **accurately** the position of the fence.

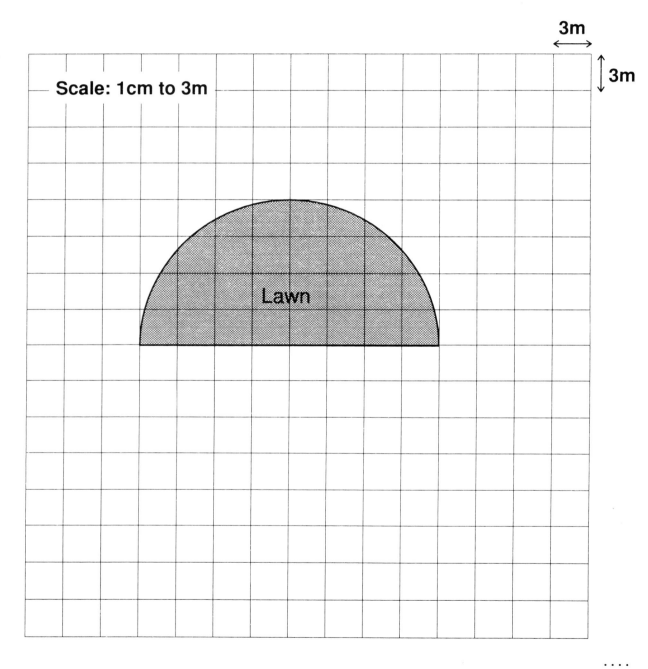

3m

3m

Scale: 1cm to 3m

Lawn

. . . .

. . . .

2 marks

This is what a pupil wrote:

For all numbers t and w,

$$\frac{1}{t} + \frac{1}{w} = \frac{2}{t + w}$$

Show that the pupil was **wrong**.

. . . .

. . . .

2 marks

22.

A customer at a supermarket complains to the manager about the waiting times at the checkouts.

The manager records the waiting times of **100 customers** at **1 checkout**.

Results

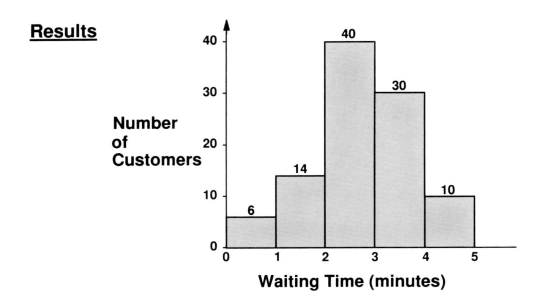

(a) Use the graph to estimate the probability that a customer chosen at random will wait for **2 minutes or longer**.

....

. . . .

1 mark

(b) Use the graph to estimate the probability that a customer chosen at random will wait for **2.5 minutes or longer**.

....

. . . .

1 mark

(c) Calculate an estimate of the **mean** waiting time per customer.
Show your working.

You may complete the table below to help you with the calculation.

Waiting Time (minutes)	Mid-point of bar (x)	Number of customers (f)	fx
0 -	0.5	6	3
1 -	1.5	14	
2 -	2.5	40	
3 -	3.5	30	
4 - 5	4.5	10	
		100	

.... minutes

. . . .

. . . .

2 marks

(d) The manager wants to improve the survey.
She records the waiting times of more customers.

Give a **different** way the manager could improve the survey.

. . . .

1 mark

(a) Find the values of a and b when p = **10**

$$a = \frac{3p^3}{2}$$

a = ...

. . . .
1 mark

$$b = \frac{2p^2(p-3)}{7p}$$

b = ...

. . . .
1 mark

(b) Simplify this expression as fully as possible:

$$\frac{3cd^2}{5cd}$$

. . . .
1 mark

(c) Multiply out and simplify these expressions:

$3(x - 2) - 2(4 - 3x)$

. . . .
1 mark

$(x + 2)(x + 3)$

. . . .
1 mark

$(x + 4)(x - 1)$

. . . .
1 mark

$(x - 2)^2$

. . . .
1 mark

24.

(a) The diagram shows the graph with equation $y = x^2$

On the same axes, sketch the graph with equation **$y = 2x^2$**

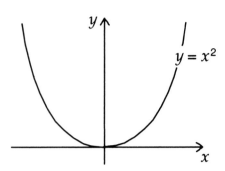

. . . .
1 mark

(b) Curve A is the reflection in the x-axis of $y = x^2$

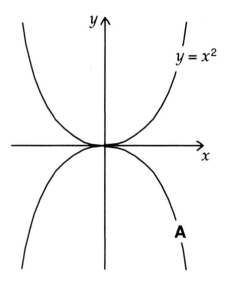

What is the equation of curve A?

. . . .
1 mark

....

(c) Curve B is the translation, one unit up the y-axis, of $y = x^2$

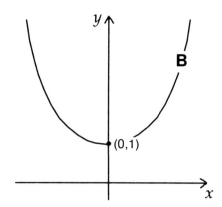

What is the equation of curve B?

....

(d) The shaded region is bounded by the curve $y = x^2$ and the line $y = 2$

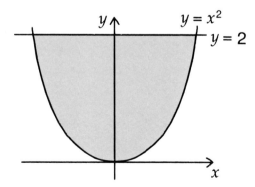

Circle **two** inequalities which together **fully describe** the shaded region.

$y < x^2$ $x < 0$ $y < 2$ $y < 0$

$y > x^2$ $x > 0$ $y > 2$ $y > 0$

. . . .

. . . .

2 marks

39

25.

(a) Which of these statements is true? Put a tick (✓) by the correct one.

4×10^3 is a larger number than 4^3 ....

4×10^3 is the same size as 4^3 ....

4×10^3 is a smaller number than 4^3 ....

Explain your answer.

. . . .
1 mark

(b) One of the numbers below has the same value as **3.6×10^4**

Put a tick (✓) under the correct number.

36^3 36^4 $(3.6 \times 10)^4$ 0.36×10^3 0.36×10^5

....

. . . .
1 mark

(c) One of the numbers below has the same value as **2.5×10^{-3}**

Put a tick (✓) under the correct number.

25×10^{-4} 2.5×10^3 -2.5×10^3 0.00025 2500

....

. . . .
1 mark

(d) $(2 \times 10^2) \times (2 \times 10^2)$ can be written more simply as 4×10^4

Write these values as simply as possible:

$(3 \times 10^2) \times (2 \times 10^{-2})$

. . . .

1 mark

$$\frac{6 \times 10^8}{2 \times 10^4}$$

. . . .

1 mark

26.

Languages

100 students were asked whether they studied French or German.

Results:

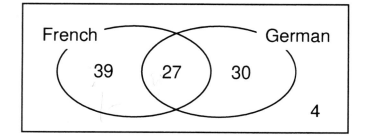

27 students studied both French **and** German.

(a) What is the probability that a student chosen at random will study only **one** of the languages?

. . . .
1 mark

(b) What is the probability that a student who is studying German is also studying French?

. /. .
1 mark

(c) Two of the 100 students are chosen at random.

Circle the calculation which shows the probability that **both** students study French and German.

$\dfrac{27}{100} \times \dfrac{26}{100}$ $\dfrac{27}{100} + \dfrac{26}{99}$ $\dfrac{27}{100} + \dfrac{27}{100}$

$\dfrac{27}{100} \times \dfrac{26}{99}$ $\dfrac{27}{100} \times \dfrac{27}{100}$

. . . .
1 mark

27.

This shape is designed using 3 semi-circles.

The radii of the semi-circles are $3a$, $2a$ and a.

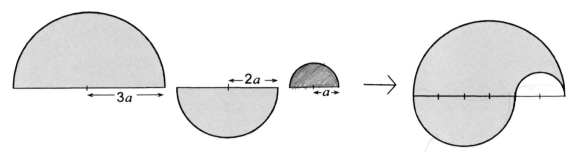

(a) Find the area of each semi-circle, in terms of a and π, and show that the **total** area of the shape is $6\pi a^2$.

. . . .

. . . .

. . . .

3 marks

(b) The area, $6\pi a^2$, of the shape is 12cm².
Write an equation in the form of $a = $ ..... , leaving your answer in terms of π.

Show your working and **simplify** your equation.

. . . .

. . . .

2 marks

END OF TEST

Combined Paper 2 Questions, 1998 Levels 3-8

Write your name and school in the spaces below.

First Name _____

Last Name _____

School _____

Remember

- Answer as many questions as you can in 1 hour. You are *not* expected to answer all the questions.

- You may use a calculator for any question in this test, if you want to.

- You will need: pen, pencil, rubber, ruler, calculator, pair of compasses, tracing paper and mirror (optional).

- Some formulae you might need are on page 3.

- This test starts with easier questions.

- Write all your answers and working on the test paper – do not use any rough paper.

- Check your work carefully.

- Ask if you are not sure what to do.

Instructions

Formulae

You might need to use these formulae.

AREA

Circle

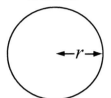

$$\pi r^2$$

Take π as 3.14

Triangle

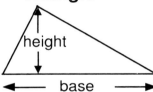

$$\frac{\text{base} \times \text{height}}{2}$$

Parallelogram

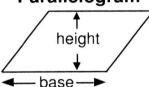

base × height

Trapezium

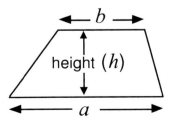

$$\frac{(a + b)}{2} \times h$$

LENGTH

Circle

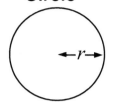

circumference = $2\pi r$

For a right-angled triangle

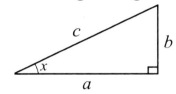

$a^2 + b^2 = c^2$ (Pythagoras' theorem)

$$a = c \cos x \qquad \cos x = \frac{a}{c}$$

$$b = c \sin x \qquad \sin x = \frac{b}{c}$$

$$b = a \tan x \qquad \tan x = \frac{b}{a}$$

VOLUME

Prism

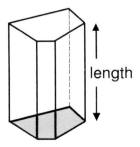

area of cross-section × length

Dan is doing a sponsored swim.
This is what Dan's friends promise to give for each length of the swimming pool he swims.

Ben says:
I will give Dan **20p** a length.

Jan says:
I will give Dan **30p** a length.

Cal says:
I will give Dan **25p** a length.

Kim says:
I will give Dan **15p** a length.

Wyn says:
I will give Dan **20p** a length.

(a)   Fill in the gaps in Dan's sponsor form.

Name	Amount for each length
Ben	20p
Cal	
	30p
	15p
	20p

. . . .

. . . .

2 marks

(b)   How much money will Dan collect altogether for each length he swims?

. . . .

1 mark

£

(c) Tom also did the sponsored swim. He swam **27** lengths.

He collected **75p** for each length.

How much money did Tom collect for the swim?

£ . . . .

1 mark

(d) Nina swam **25** lengths in the sponsored swim.

She collected **72p** for each length.

How much money did Nina collect for the swim?

£ . . . .

1 mark

Nina's mother says:

Tell me how much you collected for your swim.
I will give you a **quarter** of the amount.

How much should Nina's mother give her?

£ . . . .

1 mark

5

2.

Yen

Look at the pictures of Japanese money.

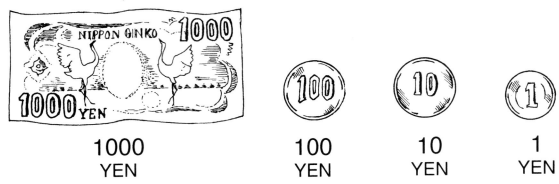

| 1000 YEN | 100 YEN | 10 YEN | 1 YEN |

Write how much is in each box.
The first is done for you.

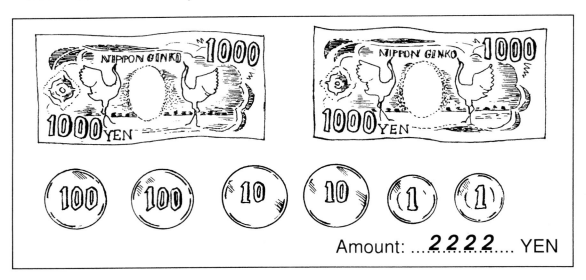

Amount: ....***2.2.2.2***.... YEN

(a)

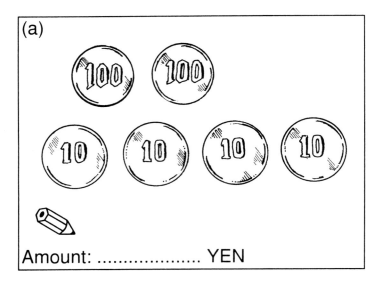

Amount: .... YEN

(b)

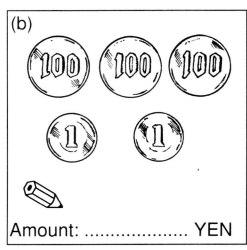

Amount: .... YEN

....
1 mark

....
1 mark

6

(b) How many **Sundays** were there altogether in **January**?

. . . .
1 mark

How many **Saturdays** were there altogether in **January**?

. . . .
1 mark

(c) There were **more Mondays** than **Thursdays** in **March**.
Complete this sentence so that it is correct:

There were more .... than .... in **April**.

. . . .
1 mark

(d) Jane went swimming on **Wednesday, January 14**.
She went swimming again **4 weeks later**.
On **what date** did she go swimming the second time?

. . . .
1 mark

(e) The swimming pool **shut** for repairs on **Friday, March 20**.
It **opened** again on **Friday, April 10**.
For **how many weeks** was the swimming pool shut?

. . . .
1 mark

(f) Which day in **March** had numbers in the **7 times table** as its dates?

. . . .
1 mark

5.

Owen has some tiles like these: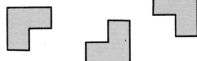

He uses the tiles to make a series of patterns.

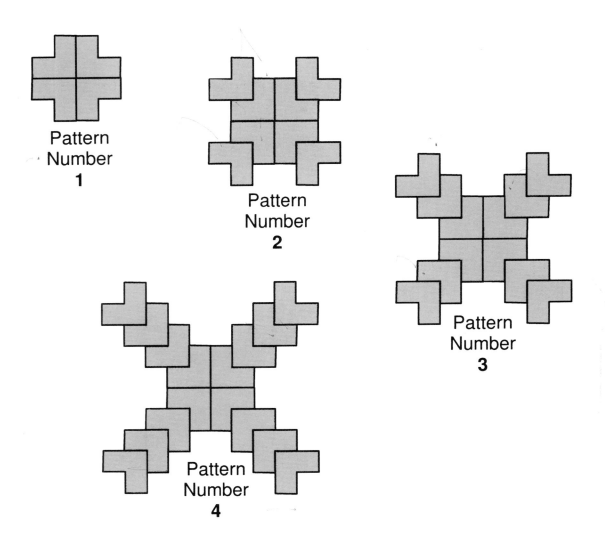

Pattern
Number
1

Pattern
Number
2

Pattern
Number
3

Pattern
Number
4

(a) Each new pattern has **more tiles** than the one before.
The number of tiles goes up by the same amount each time.

How many **more** tiles does Owen add each time he makes a new pattern?

....

1 mark

(b) **How many tiles** will Owen need altogether to make **pattern number 6**?

. . . .

1 mark

(c) **How many tiles** will Owen need altogether to make **pattern number 9**?

. . . .

1 mark

(d) Owen uses **40 tiles** to make a pattern.

What is the **number** of the **pattern** he makes?

. . . .

1 mark

6.

Here are four spinners, labelled P, Q, R and S.

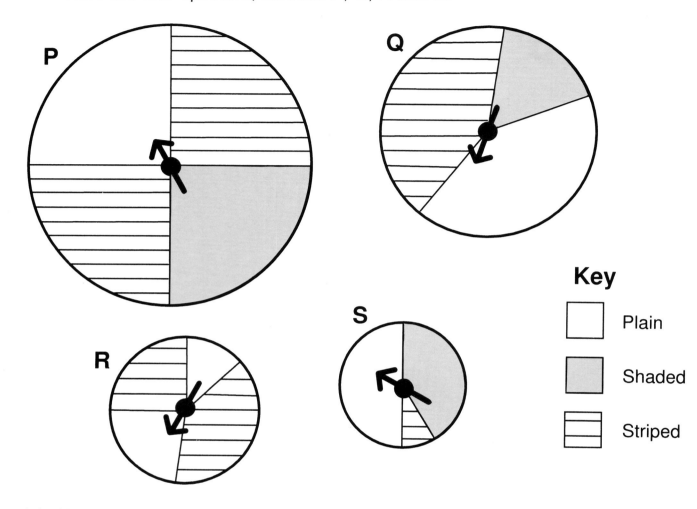

Key

☐ Plain

▨ Shaded

▤ Striped

(a) Which spinner gives the **greatest chance** that the arrow will land on **plain**?

Spinner ....

. . . .
1 mark

(b) Which spinner gives the **smallest chance** that the arrow will land on **shaded**?

Spinner ....

. . . .
1 mark

(c) Shade this spinner so that it is **certain** that the arrow will
     land on **shaded**.

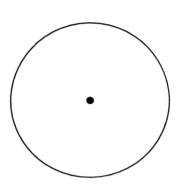

. . . .
1 mark

(d) Shade this spinner so that there is a **50% chance** that the arrow will
     land on **shaded**.

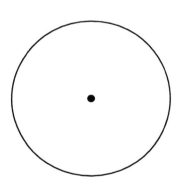

. . . .
1 mark

7.

Jim, Bob, Liz and Meg had a games competition.

They played two games, Draughts and Ludo.

Each pupil played each of the others at the two different games.

Meg recorded **how many** games each person won.

Jim	/ / /
Meg	/ / /
Liz	/ / / /
Bob	/ /

Jim recorded **who won** each game.

Draughts	*Ludo*
Jim	Meg
Liz	Bob
Bob	
Jim	Meg
Jim	Liz
Liz	Meg

(a) Jim forgot to put one of the names on his table.
Use Meg's table to work out what the missing name is.

. . . .

1 mark

(b) Who won the **most** games of **Draughts**?

. . . .

1 mark

(c) Give one reason why **Meg's** table is a good way of recording the results.

. . . .
1 mark

(d) Give one reason why **Jim's** table is a good way of recording the results.

. . . .
1 mark

8.

The table shows the lengths of some rivers to the nearest km.

(a) Write the length of each river rounded to the nearest **100km**.

River	Length in km to the nearest km	Length in km to the nearest 100 km
Severn	354	
Thames	346	
Trent	297	
Wye	215	
Dee	113	

. . . .
1 mark

Which two rivers have the **same length** to the nearest **100km**?

.... and ....

. . . .
1 mark

(b) Write the length of each river rounded to the nearest **10km**.

River	Length in km to the nearest km	Length in km to the nearest 10 km
Severn	354	
Thames	346	
Trent	297	
Wye	215	
Dee	113	

. . . .
1 mark

Which two rivers have the **same length** to the nearest **10km**?

.... and ....

. . . .
1 mark

(c) There is another river which is not on the list.

It has a length of **200km** to the **nearest 100km**,
and a length of **150km** to the **nearest 10km**.

Complete this sentence to give one possible length of the river to the nearest km.

The length of the river could be .... km.

. . . .
1 mark

(d) Two more rivers have **different** lengths to the nearest km.

They both have a length of **250km** to the **nearest 10km**,
but their lengths to the **nearest 100km** are **different**.

Complete this sentence to give a possible length of each river to the nearest km.

. . . .

. . . .

The lengths of the rivers could be .... km and .... km.

2 marks

9.

These two congruent triangles make a **parallelogram**.

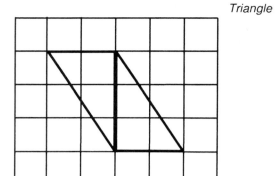

(a) Draw another congruent triangle to make a **rectangle**.

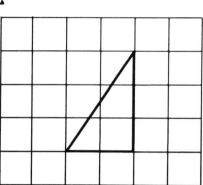

. . . .
1 mark

(b) Draw another congruent triangle to make a **bigger triangle**.

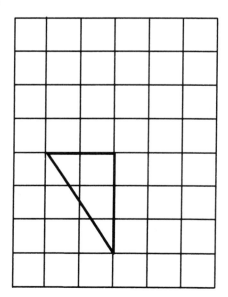

(c) Draw another congruent triangle to make a **different bigger triangle**.

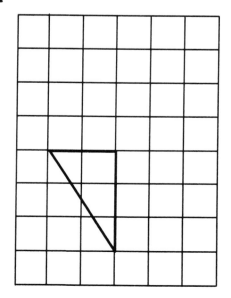

. . . .
1 mark

. . . .
1 mark

You can make different colours of paint by mixing red, blue and yellow in different **proportions**.

For example, you can make green by mixing **1 part blue** to **1 part yellow**.

(a) To make purple, you mix **3 parts red** to **7 parts blue**.

How much of each colour do you need to make **20 litres** of purple paint?

Give your answer in litres.

.... litres of red and .... litres of blue

. . . .

. . . .

2 marks

(b) To make orange, you mix **13 parts yellow** to **7 parts red**.

How much of each colour do you need to make **10 litres** of orange paint?

Give your answer in litres.

.... litres of yellow and .... litres of red

. . . .

. . . .

2 marks

11.

L-triominoes

This shape is called an **L-triomino**. It is made from three squares.

This shape is made from two L-triominoes. They do not overlap.

It has only **one line** of symmetry.

You may use a mirror or tracing paper to help you in this question.

(a) Draw a **different** shape made from two L-triominoes which do not overlap. It must have only **one line** of symmetry.

. . . .

1 mark

(b) Draw a shape made from two L-triominoes which do not overlap. It must have **two lines** of symmetry.

. . . .

1 mark

22

This shape is made from two L-triominoes which do not overlap.
It has **rotational** symmetry of order **two**.

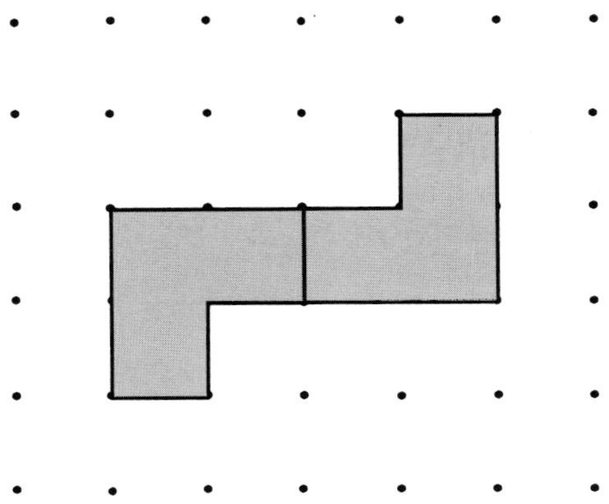

(c) Draw a **different** shape made from two L-triominoes which do not overlap.
It must have **rotational** symmetry of order **two**.

....
1 mark

(d) Draw a shape made from two L-triominoes which do not overlap.
It must have **two** lines of symmetry **and rotational** symmetry of order **two**.

....
1 mark

These pie charts show some information about the ages of people in Greece and in Ireland.

There are about 10 million people in Greece, and there are about 3.5 million people in Ireland.

Greece

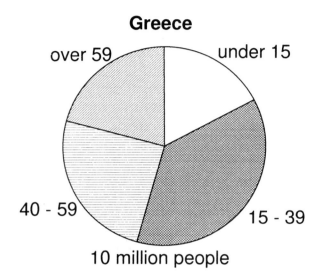

10 million people

Ireland

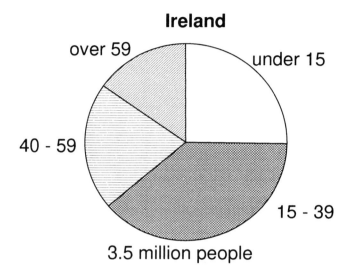

3.5 million people

(a) Roughly what **percentage** of people in **Greece** are aged **40 - 59**?

.... %

. . . .
1 mark

(b) There are about **10 million** people in Greece.
Use your percentage from part (a) to work out
roughly **how many** people in Greece are aged **40 - 59**.

.... million people

. . . .
1 mark

(c) Dewi says:

The charts show that there are **more** people **under 15** in **Ireland** than in **Greece**.

Dewi is **wrong**. Explain why the charts do **not** show this.

. . . .

1 mark

(d) There are about 60 million people in the UK.
The table shows roughly what percentage of people in the UK are of different ages.

under 15	15 - 39	40 - 59	over 59
20%	35%	25%	20%

Draw a pie chart below to show the information in the table.
Label each section of your pie chart clearly with the **ages**.

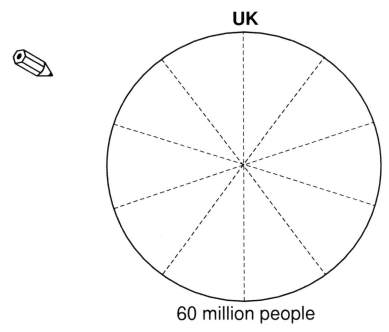

UK

60 million people

. . . .

. . . .

2 marks

. . . .

1 mark

13. *Nets*

(a) The top and the base of this box are **semi-circles**.

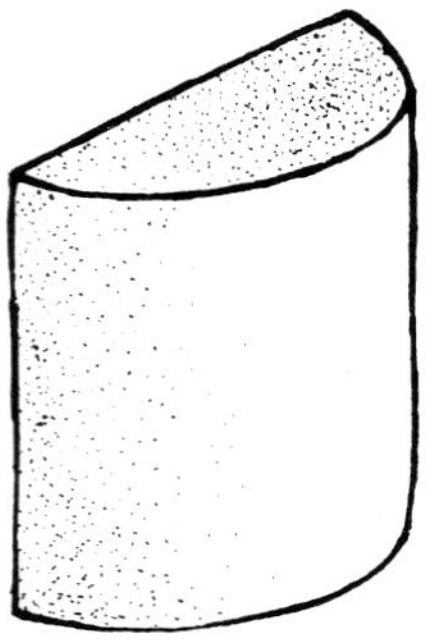

One of the nets below could fold up to make a box like this.

Put a tick (✓) on the correct net.

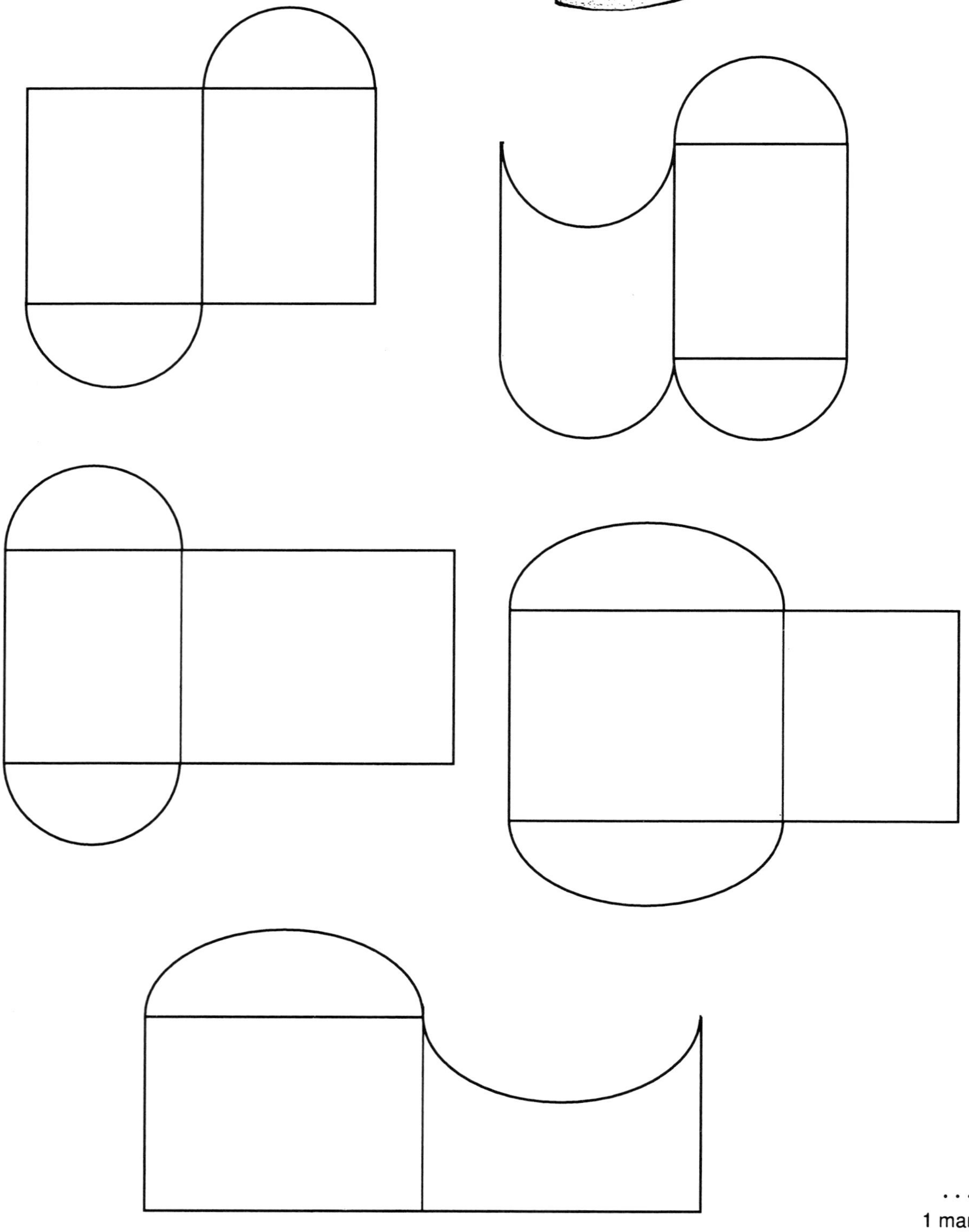

....
1 mark

(b) This is a rough sketch of the **base** of a box.
It is a **semi-circle**, with **diameter 8** cm.

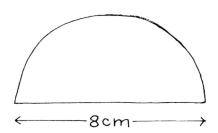

←———8cm———→

Make an accurate, full size drawing of the **base** of the box.
You will need a ruler and a pair of compasses.

. . . .

. . . .

2 marks

14.

I have two fair dice.
Each of the dice is numbered 1 to 6.

(a) The probability that I will throw
double 6 (both dice showing number 6) is

$$\frac{1}{36}$$

What is the probability that I will **not** throw double 6?

. . . .
1 mark

(b) I throw both dice and get double 6.
Then I throw the dice again.

Tick the box that describes the probability that I will throw
double 6 this time.

less than $\frac{1}{36}$ ☐

$\frac{1}{36}$ ☐

more than $\frac{1}{36}$ ☐

Explain your answer.

. . . .
1 mark

I start again and throw both dice.

(c) What is the probability that I will throw
double 3 (both dice showing number 3)?

. . . .
1 mark

(d) What is the probability that I will throw a double?
(It could be double 1 or double 2 or any other double.)

. . . .
1 mark

15.

The table shows the land area of each of the World's continents.

continent	land area (in 1 000 km²)
Africa	30 264
Antarctica	13 209
Asia	44 250
Europe	9 907
North America	24 398
Oceania	8 534
South America	17 793
World	**148 355**

(a) Which continent is approximately 12% of the World's land area?

....

. . . .
1 mark

(b) What percentage of the World's land area is **Antarctica**?
Show your working.

. . . .

. . . .
2 marks

.... %

(c) About **30%** of the World's area is **land**. The rest is water.
The amount of **land** in the World is about **150 million km²**.

Work out the approximate **total area** (land and water) of the World.
Show your working.

. . . .

. . . .
2 marks

.... million km²

Data from 'Book of Comparisons' pub. Penguin 1980

Four cubes join to make an L-shape.

The diagram shows the L-shape after **quarter turns** in one direction.

On the paper below, draw the L-shape after
the **next** quarter turn in the same direction.

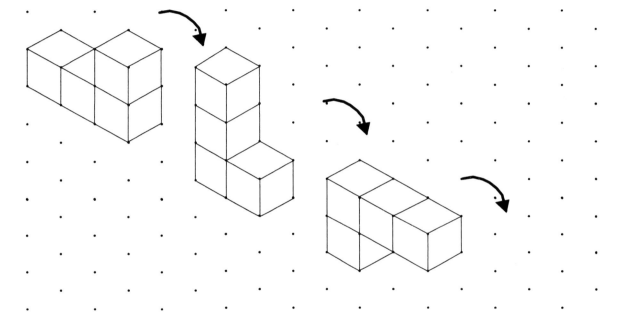

. . . .

. . . .

2 marks

17.

A competition has 3 different games.

(a) Jeff plays 2 of the games.

	Game A	Game B	Game C
Score	62	53	

To win, Jeff needs a **mean** score of **60**.

How many points does he need to score in Game C?

Show your working.

. . . .

. . . .

2 marks

. . . .

(b) Imran and Nia play the 3 games.

Their scores have the **same mean**.

The **range** of Imran's scores is **twice** the range of Nia's scores.

Fill in the missing scores in the table below:

Imran's scores	. . . .	40	. . . .
Nia's scores	35	40	45

. . . .

1 mark

The scatter diagrams show the scores of everyone who plays all 3 games.

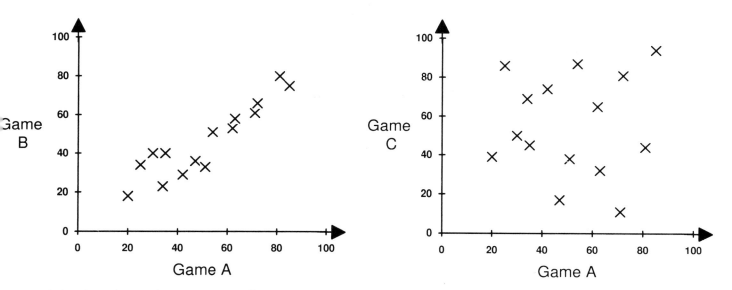

(c) Look at the scatter diagrams.
Which statement most closely describes the **relationship** between the games?

Tick (✓) the correct statement.

Game **A** and Game **B**				
perfect negative relationship	negative relationship	no relationship	positive relationship	perfect positive relationship

· · · ·
1 mark

Game **A** and Game **C**				
perfect negative relationship	negative relationship	no relationship	positive relationship	perfect positive relationship

· · · ·
1 mark

(d) What can you tell about the **relationship** between the scores on Game **B** and the scores on Game **C**?

Tick (✓) the statement that most closely describes the relationship.

Game **B** and Game **C**				
perfect negative relationship	negative relationship	no relationship	positive relationship	perfect positive relationship

· · · ·
1 mark

A box for coffee is in the shape of a hexagonal prism.

One end of the box is shown below.

Each of the 6 triangles in the hexagon has the same dimensions.

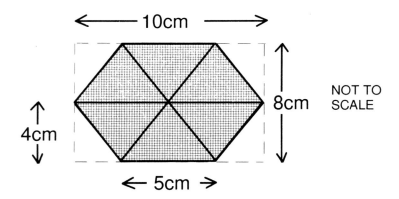

NOT TO SCALE

(a) Calculate the total **area** of the hexagon.

Show your working.

.... cm^2

. . . .

. . . .

2 marks

(b) The box is **10cm long**.

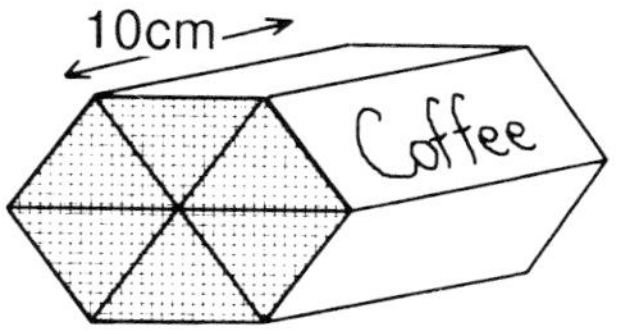

10cm → Coffee

After packing, the coffee fills **80%** of the box.

How many **grams** of coffee are in the box?
(The mass of 1cm^3 of coffee is 0.5 grams.)

Show your working.

.... grams

. . . .

. . . .

. . . .

3 marks

(c) A **227g** packet of the same coffee costs **£2.19**
How much **per 100g** of coffee is this?
Show your working.

£ ....

. . . .

. . . .

2 marks

At Winchester there is a large table known as the Round Table of King Arthur.

The **diameter** of the table is **5.5 metres**.

(a) A book claims that 50 people sat around the table.

Assume each person needs 45cm around the circumference of the table. Is it possible for 50 people to sit around the table?

Show your working to explain your answer.

. . . .

. . . .

. . . .

3 marks

(b) Assume people sitting around the table could reach only **1.5m**.

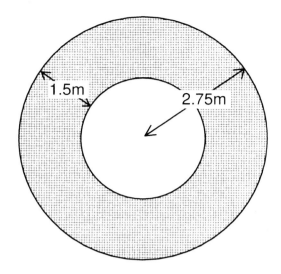

Calculate the **area** of the table that could be reached.

Show your working.

.... m²

. . . .

. . . .

. . . .

3 marks

20.

Some pupils threw 3 fair dice.

They recorded how many times the numbers on the dice were the same.

Name	Number of throws	Results		
		all different	2 the same	all the same
Morgan	40	26	12	2
Sue	140	81	56	3
Zenta	20	10	10	0
Ali	100	54	42	4

(a) Write the name of the pupil whose data are **most likely** to give the best estimate of the probability of getting each result.

....

Explain your answer.

(b) This table shows the pupils' results collected together:

Number of throws	Results		
	all different	2 the same	all the same
300	171	120	9

Use these data to estimate the **probability** of throwing numbers that are **all different**.

(c) The theoretical probability of each result is shown below:

	all different	2 the same	all the same
Probability	$\dfrac{5}{9}$	$\dfrac{5}{12}$	$\dfrac{1}{36}$

Use these probabilities to calculate, for 300 throws, **how many times** you would theoretically expect to get each result.

Number	Theoretical results		
of throws	all different	2 the same	all the same
300	....	....	....

. . . .

. . . .

2 marks

(d) Explain why the pupils' results are not the same as the theoretical results.

. . . .

1 mark

(e) Jenny throws the 3 dice twice.

Calculate the probability that she gets **all the same** on her first throw and gets **all the same** on her second throw.

Show your working.

. . . .

. . . .

2 marks

21.

> In this question you will get no marks if you
> work out the answers through scale drawing.

(a) Cape Point is 7.5km east and 4.8km north of Arton.

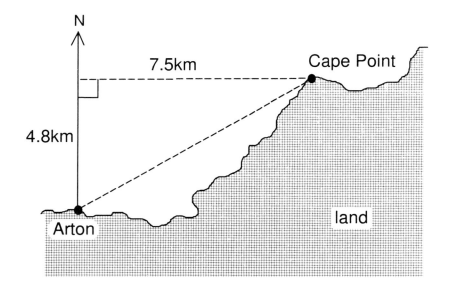

Calculate the direct distance from Arton to Cape Point.
Show your working.

.... km

. . . .

. . . .

2 marks

Bargate is 6km east and 4km north of Cape Point.

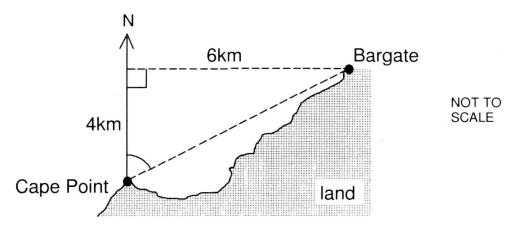

NOT TO SCALE

(b) Steve wants to sail directly from Cape Point to Bargate.
On what bearing should he sail?

Show your working.

....
....
2 marks

..............°

(c) Anna sails from Cape Point on a bearing of 048°.
She stops when she is due north of Bargate.

How far north of Bargate is Anna?

Show your working.

....
....
....
3 marks

.... km

22.

Look at the table:

Birth rate per 1000 population

	1961	1994
England	17.6	
Wales	17.0	12.2

(a) In England, from 1961 to 1994, the birth rate **fell** by 26.1%.
What was the birth rate in England in 1994?

Show your working.

....

. . . .

. . . .

2 marks

(b) In Wales, the birth rate also fell.
Calculate the **percentage fall** from 1961 to 1994.

Show your working.

.... %

. . . .

. . . .

2 marks

(c) From 1961 to 1994, the birth rates in Scotland and Northern Ireland fell by the **same** amount.

The **percentage fall** in Scotland was greater than the percentage fall in Northern Ireland.

Put a tick (✓) by the statement below which is true.

In 1961, the birth rate in Scotland was **higher** than the birth rate in Northern Ireland.	....
In 1961, the birth rate in Scotland was **the same as** the birth rate in Northern Ireland.	....
In 1961, the birth rate in Scotland was **lower** than the birth rate in Northern Ireland.	....
From the information given, you cannot tell whether Scotland or Northern Ireland had the higher birth rate in 1961.	....

. . . .
1 mark

The cumulative frequency graph shows the height of 150 Norway fir trees.

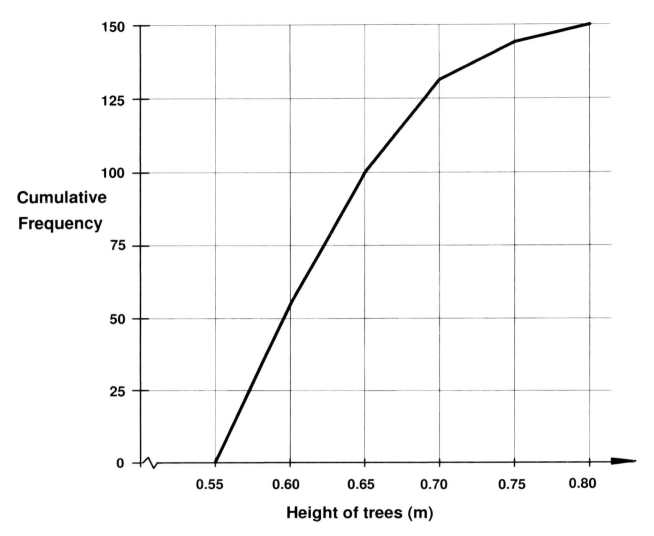

(a) Use the graph to estimate the **median** height and the **interquartile range** of the Norway firs.

median = ... m

. . . .
1 mark

interquartile range = ... m

. . . .
. . . .
2 marks

(b) One of these sketches shows the distribution of heights of the Norway firs.
Put a tick (✓) by the side of the correct frequency diagram.

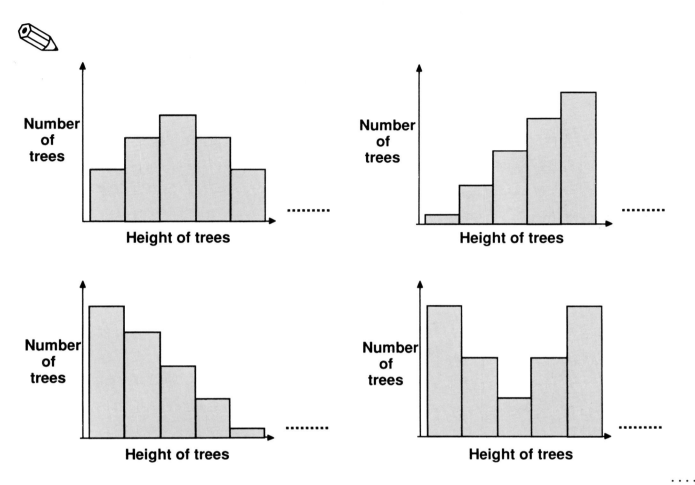

. . . .

1 mark

These plant pots are mathematically similar.
The internal dimensions are shown.

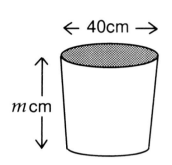

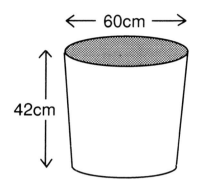

NOT TO
SCALE

(a)   Calculate the value of *m*.

Show your working.

m = ... cm

. . . .

. . . .

2 marks

(b) The capacity, C, of a plant pot in **cubic centimetres** is given by the formula:

$$C = \frac{1}{12}\pi h(a^2 + ab + b^2)$$

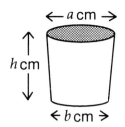

In the larger plant pot $a = 60$, $b = 36$ and $h = 42$

How many **litres** of compost are needed to fill the plant pot?

Show your working.

.... litres

. . . .

. . . .

. . . .

3 marks

(c) Think about the ratio of the widths of the two plant pots.

Explain why the ratio of the capacity of the smaller pot to the capacity of the larger pot is **8 : 27**

. . . .

1 mark

END OF TEST

Mark Scheme for Papers 1 and 2, 1998 Levels 3–8

Introduction

This guidance on marking is provided to help parents in assessing their child's answers to the questions. It includes the mark scheme for papers 1 and 2 at Levels 3-8. Questions have been given names so that each one has a unique identifier along with its number.

The structure of the mark scheme

The marking information for questions is set out in the form of tables, which start on page 7. The column on the left hand side of each table provides a quick reference to the question number, question part, and the total number of marks available for that question part.

The **'Correct response'** column usually includes two types of information:

- a statement of the requirements for the award of each mark,
  with an indication of whether credit can be given for correct working,
  and whether the marks are independent or cumulative;

- examples of some different types of correct response,
  including the most common and the minimum acceptable.

The **'Additional guidance'** column indicates alternative acceptable responses, and provides details of specific types of response which are unacceptable. Other guidance, such as when 'follow through' is allowed, is provided as necessary.

For graphical and diagrammatic responses, including those in which degrees of accuracy are hard to judge, marking overlays have been provided in a separate pad (see inside back cover).

Using the mark schemes

Answers that are numerically equivalent or algebraically equivalent are acceptable unless the marks scheme states otherwise. The most frequent procedural queries are listed below with the prescribed correct action. Unless otherwise specified in the mark scheme, you should apply the following guidelines in all cases.

What if . . .

My child's response does not match closely any of the examples given.	You should use your judgement in deciding whether the response corresponds with the statement of requirements given in the 'Correct response' column.
My child has responded in a non-standard way.	Calculations, formulae and written responses do not have to be set out in any particular format. Your child may provide evidence in any form as long as its meaning can be understood. Diagrams, symbols or words are acceptable for explanations or for indicating a response. Any correct method of setting out working, however idiosyncratic, is acceptable.
My child's accuracy is marginal according to the overlay provided.	Overlays can never be 100% accurate. However, provided the answer is within, or touches, the boundaries given, the mark(s) should be awarded. If still in doubt you should check with appropriate measuring equipment.
My child's answer correctly follows through from earlier incorrect work.	'Follow through' marks may be awarded only when specifically stated in the mark scheme, but should not be allowed if the difficulty level of the question has been lowered. *Either the correct response or an acceptable 'follow through' response should be marked as correct.*
There appears to be a misreading affecting the working.	This is when your child misreads the information given in the question and uses different information without altering the original intention or difficulty level of the question. For each misread that occurs, deduct one mark only
The correct answer is in the wrong place.	Where your child has shown understanding of the question, the mark(s) should be given. In particular, where a word or number response is expected, your child may meet the requirement by annotating a graph or labelling a diagram elsewhere in the question.

The final answer is wrong but the correct answer is shown in the working.	Where appropriate, detailed guidance will be given in the mark scheme, and must be adhered to. If no guidance is given, you will need to examine each case to decide whether:	
	the incorrect answer is due to a transcription error;	If so, award the mark.
	in questions not testing accuracy, the correct answer has been given but then rounded or truncated;	If so, award the mark.
	your child has continued to give redundant extra working which *does not* contradict work already done.	If so, award the mark.
	your child has continued to give redundant extra working which *does* contradict work already done.	If so, *do not* award the mark.
My child's answer is correct but the wrong working is seen.	A correct response should always be marked as correct unless the mark scheme states otherwise.	
The correct response has been crossed (or rubbed) out and not replaced.	Mark, according to the mark scheme, any legible crossed (or rubbed) out work that has been replaced.	
More than one answer is given.	If all answers given are correct (or a range of answers are given, all of which are correct), the mark should be awarded unless prohibited by the mark scheme. *If both correct and incorrect responses are given no mark should be awarded.*	
The answer is correct but, in a later part of the question my child has contradicted this response.	A mark given for one part should not be disallowed for working or answers given in a different part, unless the mark scheme specifically states otherwise.	

General guidance

Throughout the marking of the Key Stage 3 mathematics tests, the following general guidelines should be observed unless specific instructions to the contrary are given. This guidance reflects decisions made to ensure fairness and consistency of marking.

Responses involving probability

A numerical probability should be expressed as a decimal, fraction, or percentage only.

	Accept	Do not accept
For example: 0.7	✓ A correct probability that is correctly expressed as a decimal, fraction or percentage, even if it is accompanied by the same probability incorrectly expressed eg 0.7 or 7 in 10, $\quad$ 7 out of 10 $= \frac{7}{10}$, $\quad$ 7 in 10 = 70%, $\quad \frac{7}{10} = 7 : 10$, $\quad$ 7 : 3 or 70% ✓ Equivalent decimals, fractions or percentages eg 0.700, $\frac{70}{100}$, $\frac{35}{50}$, 70.0% ✓ A probability correctly expressed in one acceptable form which is then incorrectly converted, but is still less than 1 and greater than 0 eg $\frac{70}{100} = \frac{18}{25}$	✗ A probability that is incorrectly expressed eg 7 in 10, 7 out of 10, $\quad$ 7 from 10 ✗ A probability expressed as a percentage without a percentage sign. ✗ A fraction with other than integers in the numerator and/or denominator. However, to avoid penalising any of these three types of error more than once within each question, deduct only the mark for the *first* occurrence of each type within each question. ✗ A probability expressed as a ratio eg 7 : 10, 7 : 3, 7 to 10 ✗ A probability greater than 1 or less than 0

Responses involving money

	Accept	Do not accept
For example: £3.20	✓ Any unambiguous indication of the correct amount eg £3.20(p), £3 20, £3,20, 3 pounds 20, £3-20, £3 20pence, £3:20 ✓ The £ sign is usually already printed in the answer space. Where the pupil writes an answer other than in the answer space, or crosses out the £ sign, accept an answer with correct units in pounds and/or pence eg 320p	✗ Incorrect or ambiguous use of pounds or pence eg £320, £320p, 3.20 or 3.20p not in answer space ✗ Incorrect placement of decimal points, spaces, etc or incorrect use or omission of 0 eg £3.2, £3 200, £32 0, £3-2-0

Responses involving the use of algebra

	Accept	Do not accept
For example: 2 + *n* *n* + 2 2*n*	✓ The unambiguous use of a different case eg *N* used for *n* ✓ Unconventional notation for multiplication eg *n* × 2 or 2 × *n* or *n*2 or *n* + *n* for 2*n*, *n* × *n* for n^2 ✓ Multiplication by 1 or 0 eg 2 + 1*n* for 2 + *n*, 2 + 0*n* for 2 ✓ Words used to precede or follow equations or expressions eg *t* = *n* + 2 tiles or tiles = *t* = *n* + 2 for *t* = *n* + 2 ✓ Unambiguous letters used to indicate expressions eg *t* = *n* + 2 for *n* + 2 ✓ Embedded values given when solving equations eg 3 × 10 + 2 = 32 for 3*x* + 2 = 32	✗ Change of variable eg *x* used for *n* ✗ Words or units used within equations or expressions eg *n* tiles + 2 *n* cm + 2 ✗ Ambiguous letters used to indicate expressions eg *n* = *n* + 2 However, to avoid penalising any of these three types of error more than once within each question, deduct only the mark for the *first* occurrence of each type within each question. ✗ Embedded values that are then contradicted eg for 3*x* + 2 = 32, 3 × 10 + 2 = 32, *x* = 5

[Blank page]

Marks		Question 1	Bus
		Correct response	**Additional guidance**

1m	a	Indicates 09:15	*Throughout the question* ignore any reference to am or pm.
			
			Accept any indication
			eg
			    'Quarter past nine.'
			    '915'
			    '9-15'

1m		Indicates 45	Accept any indication
			eg
			    'Three quarters of an hour.'
			    '00:45'

1m	b	Indicates the correct bus eg ■ '09:30' ■ '10-15' ■ 'The third bus.' ■ 'Half past 9' ■ '930' ■ Arrow drawn to correct bus.	
1m	c	Indicates £11 eg ■ '11' in answer space. ■ '11.00' in answer space. ■ '£11'	

Mark Scheme Paper 1

Marks		Question 2	Angles
		Correct response	**Additional guidance**
1m	a	Indicates the two correct angles, and no other angles eg 	Accept any indication eg Angle sizes marked, with correct pair equal or within four degrees of each other.
1m	b	Draws an angle which is greater than 90°.	Angles need not be accurately drawn provided the pupil's intention is clear. Accept a reflex angle which is clearly indicated. Accept a straight line in which the 180° angle is clearly indicated. Ignore any attempt to label the angle size.
1m	c	Indicates South eg ▪ 'S' ▪ Draws an arrow down the page.	**Do not accept** ambiguous or incorrect indications eg 'Down'
1m	d	Indicates South	

Marks		Question 3	Stations
		Correct response	**Additional guidance**
1m	a	Indicates 20 miles eg ▪ '20 miles' ▪ '20 m'	The correct units must be given at least once within this question. If they are not given anywhere in the question, **do not accept** the last response which is otherwise correct and would have been awarded the mark.
1m	b	Indicates 53 miles.	
1m	c	Indicates 9 miles.	

Marks		Question 4	Symmetry
		Correct response	**Additional guidance**
1m		Draws the correct line, and no other lines eg ■ 	Drawings need not be accurate and lines of symmetry need not extend to the edge of the pattern, provided the pupil's intention is clear.
1m		Draws the four correct lines, and no other lines eg ■ 	
1m		Draws the three correct lines, and no other lines eg ■ 	

Mark Scheme Paper 1

Marks		Question 5	Cuboids
		Correct response	**Additional guidance**
1m	a	Indicates 10	
1m		Indicates 16	
1m		Indicates 30	
1m	b	Indicates 24	

Marks		Question 6	Calculations
		Correct response	**Additional guidance**
1m	a	Indicates a pair of numbers with a sum of 34	
1m		Indicates a pair of numbers with a product of 10	
1m	b	Indicates 12	**Do not accept** remainders other than 0.
1m	c	Indicates 275	
1m		Indicates 368	
1m		Indicates 16	**Do not accept** remainders other than 0.

Marks		Question 7 Correct response	Cassettes Additional guidance
1m	a	Indicates £40	*Throughout the question,* ignore any reference to money left over, even if it is incorrect.
1m	b	Indicates £5.96	
1m	c	Indicates 8	
1m	d	Indicates 3	Accept 9 (cassettes).

1m	e	Indicates 11
		eg
		  ■ '11'
		  ■ 'Three packs (of three) and two singles.'
		  ■ '3 × 3 + 2'
		  ■ '3 at £3.99 and 2 at £1.49'
			Accept indication of the total cost
			eg
			   '£14.95'
			   '£11.97 + £2.98'
			
			Ignore references to five items bought if it is clear from the working that three of these are packs (at £3.99) and two are cassettes (at £1.49)

Marks		Question 8 Correct response	Magic Squares Additional guidance
1m		Indicates 63 as total.	For each cell, **allow follow through** from an incorrect total found, **provided** the two relevant values given in the square have been used.
1m		Indicates 21 in centre cell.	Accept the difference between the pupil's total and 42
1m		Indicates 40 in centre right cell.	Accept the difference between the pupil's total and 23
1m		Indicates 8 in bottom centre cell. eg for 4m ■	Accept the difference between the pupil's total and 55

Marks		Question 9	Cakes
		Correct response	**Additional guidance**

1m	a	Indicates the correct mass in grams for all three items
		eg
		■ '1000 g caster sugar
		  1500 g margarine
		  1250 g mixed fruit'	

2m		**For 2m** indicates the correct mass in kilograms of all three items
		eg
		■ '1 kg caster sugar
		  1.5 kg margarine
		  $1\frac{1}{4}$ kg mixed fruit'
		
		For only 1m indicates the correct mass in kilograms of any two items.
			Accept unrounded masses in kilograms given to any number of decimal places
			eg
			  '1.000 kg; 1.50 kg; 1.25 kg'
			
			Accept correct masses in kilograms and grams, with units indicated correctly
			eg
			  '1 kg 500'
			  '1 kilo 250g'
			
			For 2m or only 1m, allow follow through from their number of grams provided three different masses have been given, not more than one of which is a whole number of kilograms, and at least one of which has three or more non-zero digits.

1m	b	Indicates £3.50	

Mark Scheme Paper 1

Marks		Question 10	Jigsaw
		Correct response	**Additional guidance**

1m	a	Indicates 4 corner
		            12 edge
		            8 middle	

2m	b	**For 2m** indicates 4 corner
		                       18 edge
		                       20 middle
		
		 For only 1m indicates two of the three numbers correctly.
		 or
		 Indicates the correct numbers in the wrong order.
			Note that this part does not appear in the tier 5-7 paper.

2m	c	**For 2m** indicates 4 corner
		                       32 edge
		
		             100 total
		
		 For only 1m indicates two of the three numbers correctly.	

Mark Scheme Paper 1

Marks		Question 11	Headwork
		Correct response	**Additional guidance**

2m	a	**For 2m** completes the chart correctly
		eg
		■ 10% of 240 is **24**
		   5% of 240 is **12**
		   $2\frac{1}{2}$ % of 240 is **6**
		   so $17\frac{1}{2}$ % of 240 is **42**
		
		For only 1m shows a complete method for finding $17\frac{1}{2}$ %
		eg
		■ Shows 10%, 5% and $2\frac{1}{2}$ %
		
		■ Shows (5%), 15% and $2\frac{1}{2}$ %
		
		■ Shows 10%, 20% and 5% totalled, then halves.
		
		■ Shows 10%, 7% and $\frac{1}{2}$ %
		
		■ Shows (10%), 20%, then subtracts $2\frac{1}{2}$ %
		
		or
		Indicates that the total percentage of 240 is 42, without showing a complete method.
			For 2m also accept alternative methods leading to a total of $17\frac{1}{2}$ % of 240
			eg
			   5% of 240 is **12**
			   15% of 240 is **36**
			   $2\frac{1}{2}$ % of 240 is **6**
			   so $17\frac{1}{2}$ % of 240 is **42**
			
			   20% of 240 is **48**
			   10% of 240 is **24**
			   5% of 240 is **12**
			   Halve it.
			So $17\frac{1}{2}$ % of 240 is **42**
			
			   10% of 240 is **24**
			   7% of 240 is **16.8**
			   0.5% of 240 is **1.2**
			   so $17\frac{1}{2}$ % of 240 is **42**
			
			   20% of 240 is **48**
			   $2\frac{1}{2}$ % of 240 is **6**
			   so $17\frac{1}{2}$ % of 240 is **42**
			
			For 2m or only 1m accept the rows of the chart showing the method in any order
			eg
			   5% of 240 is **12**
			   10% of 240 is **24**
			   $2\frac{1}{2}$ % of 240 is **6**
			   so $17\frac{1}{2}$ % of 240 is **42**
			
			For 2m or only 1m do not accept methods which do not show how $17\frac{1}{2}$ % of 240 is to be found
			eg
			   Percentages summing to 35% shown, with no indication that the result must be halved. 10%, 5% and 15% shown, with no indication that $2\frac{1}{2}$ % is also required.
			
			For only 1m also accept the chart completed correctly but the percentage sign incorrectly used in the second column.

14

Marks		Question 14	Quiz
		Correct response	**Additional guidance**
2m	a	**For 2m** indicates classes Q, R and T only. **For only 1m** indicates two correct classes, and not more than one incorrect class. **or** Indicates three correct classes and one incorrect class.	Accept any indication. Accept the correct classes indicated in any order.
2m	b	**For 2m** indicates the second and fourth statements only eg ■ **For only 1m** indicates one correct statement and no incorrect statements. **or** Indicates both correct statements and one incorrect statement.	**Allow follow through** from part (a) provided exactly three graphs were selected. The only valid follow through is for the second statement to be taken as false, so if the pupil has selected three classes including class P or class S, then **for 2m** accept: **For only 1m** accept: Accept any indication provided the pupil's intention is clear. If a mixture of ticks, crosses and blanks are used, assume that only the ticks indicate selections.
1m	c	Completes the graph to show a mean score of 6 eg ■ ■	Drawings need not be accurate provided the pupil's intention is clear. The total sum of the products of each score drawn with its percentage must equal 70. **Do not accept** a graph in which more or less than 100% of pupils are shown.

Marks		Question 15	Water
		Correct response	**Additional guidance**
1m 1m 1m		Indicates, for graphs 1, 2 and 3 respectively, C A E	Accept any non-ambiguous indication such as numbers used to indicate the containers.

Marks		Question 16	Lines
		Correct response	**Additional guidance**
1m	a	Indicates the correct line eg ■ '$x = 8$' ■ '$8 = x$'	*Throughout the question* accept equivalent equations eg for $y = x + 7$, accept '$x + 10 - 3 = y$'
1m	b	Indicates the correct line eg ■ '$y = x + 7$' ■ '$x = y - 7$' ■ '$y - x = 7$'	*Throughout the question* do not accept responses not given as equations eg 'x is 8'
1m	c	Indicates the correct line eg ■ '$y = x - 1$' ■ '$y = x + - 1$' ■ '$x = y + 1$' ■ '$y + 4 = x + 3$'	

Mark Scheme Paper 1

Marks		Question 17	Area
		Correct response	**Additional guidance**
1m	a	Gives a correct value eg ■ '2.5'	Accept equivalent fractions and decimals.
1m	b	Gives a correct value eg ■ '10'	**Do not accept** 10 written other than on the answer line unless it is clear that the 10 is not referring to the given area.
1m	c	Indicates values for h, a and b such that $(a + b) \times h = 20$ **and** $a > b$	The following most common responses may be helpful when marking: $\begin{array}{c\|c} h & a+b \\ \hline 1 & 20 \\ 2 & 10 \\ 2.5 & 8 \\ 3\frac{1}{3} & 6 \\ 4 & 5 \\ 5 & 4 \\ 10 & 2 \\ 20 & 1 \end{array}$ Accept $3\frac{1}{3}$ truncated to 3.3, or better. **Do not accept** negative values or zero.
1m		Indicates different values for h, a and b such that $(a + b) \times h = 20$ **and** $a > b$	Any *one* value may be the same as the previous response. If both sets of values are otherwise correct but $a \not> b$, this second mark may be given.
2m	d	**For 2m** indicates the length and width eg ■ 'length = 4cm, width = 2.5cm' **For only 1m** shows a correct value for x eg ■ '0.5' **or** Shows the length of the rectangle is 4cm. **or** Shows a complete correct method to find the length **and** width with only one computational error.	Accept length and width in either order. **For 1m** accept the length or width shown as 0.5 The one error may lead to more complex values for the length or width. Accept decimals which are rounded or truncated to 1 or more d.p.

Marks		Question 18	Tiles
		Correct response	**Additional guidance**
2m	a	For **2m** gives all 4 correct values eg ▪ <table><tr><td>5</td><td>6</td><td>10</td></tr><tr><td>16</td><td>17</td><td>32</td></tr></table> For only **1m** gives any 2 or 3 correct values. or Gives all 4 values but transposes the colours eg ▪ <table><tr><td>5</td><td>10</td><td>6</td></tr><tr><td>16</td><td>32</td><td>17</td></tr></table>	Ignore any reference to colour eg, accept '6g, 10w'
2m	b	For **2m** gives 2 correct expressions eg ▪ |	grey	white
---	---	---
n	$n+1$	$2n$ | ▪ |	grey	white
---	---	---

n	$2n-(n-1)$	$n+n$ |
		
		For only **1m** gives 1 correct expression.
		or
		Gives 2 correct expressions using words or multiple letters
		eg
		▪ 'Pattern number + 1' for grey,
		  'double the pattern number' for white.
		▪ '1 + pn' for grey, '2pn' for white.
		or
		Gives 2 correct expressions in the wrong order, even though no evidence of incorrect ordering has been shown in (a).
			For **2m or 1m** accept correct expressions for (b) given in (c)
			eg
			  for 2m: '+1, ×2' in (b), '$n+1$, $2n$' in (c)
			  for 2m: no response in (b), '$n+1$, $2n$' in (c)
			  for 2m: 'g, w' in (b), '$g = n+1$, $w = 2n$' in (c)
			
			For **2m or 1m allow follow through** from part (a) for each column independently, **provided** the difficulty level has not been decreased. One of the columns must at least be of the form $n + k$ ($k \neq 0$). The other must be different and at least of the form an ($a \neq 1$ or 0)
			eg, for 2m
			<table><tr><td>5</td><td>4</td><td>12</td></tr><tr><td>16</td><td>15</td><td>34</td></tr><tr><td>n</td><td>$n-1$</td><td>$2n+2$</td></tr></table> <table><tr><td>5</td><td>3</td><td>15</td></tr><tr><td>16</td><td>14</td><td>48</td></tr><tr><td>n</td><td>$n-2$</td><td>$3n$</td></tr></table>
			eg, for 1m
			<table><tr><td>5</td><td>7</td><td>8</td></tr><tr><td>16</td><td>18</td><td>19</td></tr><tr><td>n</td><td>$n+2$</td><td>$n+3$</td></tr></table>
			eg, **do not accept**
			<table><tr><td>5</td><td>5</td><td>12</td></tr><tr><td>16</td><td>16</td><td>32</td></tr><tr><td>n</td><td>n</td><td>$2n+2$</td></tr></table>

Marks		Question 18 (cont)	Tiles (cont)
		Correct response	**Additional guidance**

1m	c	Indicates a correct, simplified expression
		eg
		■ '3*n* + 1'
		■ '1 + *n* × 3'
			Allow follow through from two algebraic expressions given in part (b), **provided** they are able to be simplified
			eg
			    accept '2*n* + 3' from *n* + 1 and *n* + 2
			    but not '*n*² + *n* + 1' from *n* + 1 and *n*².
			
			Throughout the question ignore redundant brackets
			eg
			    '4 + (5*n*)'
			but **do not accept** incorrect brackets
			eg
			    '(4 + 5)*n*'

2m	d	**For 2m** indicates a correct, simplified expression eg ■ '5*n* + 4' ■ '4 + *n* × 5' **For only 1m** indicates a correct but unsimplified expression eg ■ '2*n* + 2 + 3*n* + 2' ■ '*n* + *n* + 1 + *n* + 2 + *n* + 1 + *n*' ■ '9 + 5(*n* − 1)' ■ '$\frac{10n}{2} + 4$' **or** Indicates correct expressions for the number of grey and white tiles separately, even if unsimplified eg ■ 'grey = 2*n* + 2 and white = 3*n* + 2' ■ 'grey = 2(*n* + 1), white = *n* + *n* + 2 + *n*' ■ '*n* + 1 + *n* + 1, 2*n* + *n* + 2' **or** Indicates correct expressions for each column eg ■ '*n*, *n* + 1, *n* + 2, *n* + 1, *n*' **or** Gives a simplified expression of the form 5*n* ± k where k is any integer including zero eg ■ '9 + 5 × *n*'	

Mark Scheme Paper 1

Marks		Question 19	Sixty
		Correct response	**Additional guidance**
1m	a	Indicates 250	**Do not accept** responses which include operations eg '6 ÷ 6 × 60'
1m		Indicates (0).1 or $\frac{1}{10}$	Accept equivalent fractions or decimals.

1m	b	Indicates $a = 20$	**Do not accept** redundant information, ambiguous responses or partial evaluation
			eg
			    '$a = \times\ 20$'
			    '$a = 100 \div 5$'
			    '$b = 5-$'
			    '$c = 6^2$'

1m		Indicates $b = -5$	
1m		Indicates $c = 6$ or -6 **or both.**	
3m	c	**For 3m** indicates $x = 20$ and $y = 5$	**For 3m** accept embedded values only if they are embedded in both the given equations eg '$20 + 8 \times 5\ (= 60)$; $4 \times 20 - 4 \times 5\ (= 60)$'

		For only 2m gives only one of the correct values for x or y.
		or
		Gives values for x and y that satisfy one of the original equations **and** shows a complete and correct algebraic method with only one error.
			For 2m accept embedded values given in only one of the equations provided no other embedded values are also indicated.
			
			For 2m values for x and y need not be integers. The other positive integral solutions for x, y that satisfy $x + 8y = 60$ are:
			    4, 7 12, 6 28, 4 36, 3
			    44, 2 52, 1 60, 0
			Solutions for $4x - 4y = 60$ are such that
			    $y = x - 15$

		For only 1m shows the correct multiplication of one of the equations by any constant eg ■ '$4x + 32y = 240$' ■ '$8x - 8y = 120$' ■ '$x - y = 15$' **or** Gives values for x and y that satisfy one of the original equations. **or** Correctly rearranges one of the given equations eg ■ '$x = 60 - 8y$' ■ '$4x = 60 + 4y$' ■ '$x = (60 + 4y) \div 4$' ■ '$4y = 4x - 60$' **or** Correctly equates both equations and simplifies to 2 terms eg ■ '$12y = 3x$' ■ '$- 4y + x = 0$'	

Mark Scheme Paper 1

Marks		Question 20 Marking overlay provided	Locus
		Correct response	**Additional guidance**
2m		**For 2m** completes the whole locus correctly, within the tolerance shown on the overlay. **For only 1m** draws the locus correctly at least between points A and B, **and** at least between points C and D, even if the remaining locus is omitted or outside the given tolerance eg • • • **or** Draws the 2 quarter-circles at least between points P and Q, **and** at least between points R and S, even if the remaining locus is omitted or outside the given tolerance eg • **or** Completes the whole locus correctly, ± 2mm, but consistently uses a wrong scale.	Accept lines drawn freehand, provided they are within the given tolerance. If the locus is shown as a set of points, and there are sufficient to illustrate the whole locus, award only 1m. Points A, B, C, D, P, Q, R and S are shown on the overlay and below.

Marks		Question 21	Numbers
		Correct response	**Additional guidance**
2m		**For 2m** gives a correct justification, either through the use of a counter-example or algebraically. The most common types of response are shown below. Use of a counter-example: Chooses values for t and w, then does one of the following: Substitutes into $\dfrac{2}{t+w}$ and correctly adds their chosen fractions, showing that they give different values eg ■ '$\dfrac{1}{2}+\dfrac{1}{2}=\dfrac{2}{4}$ but it should be 1' ■ '$\dfrac{1}{2}+\dfrac{1}{4}=\dfrac{3}{4}$ not $\dfrac{2}{6}$' ■ '$\dfrac{1}{5}+\dfrac{1}{5}=0.2+0.2=0.4$ but $\dfrac{2}{10}=0.2$'	Accept $t = w$. Accept decimals rounded or truncated. Accept implicit indication that the values are not the same eg '$\dfrac{1}{6}+\dfrac{1}{7}=\dfrac{2}{13}, \dfrac{1}{6}+\dfrac{1}{7}=\dfrac{7}{42}+\dfrac{6}{42}=\dfrac{13}{42}$' For 2m **do not accept** correct addition or substitution followed by incorrect processing eg '$\dfrac{1}{6}+\dfrac{1}{7}=\dfrac{7+6}{42}=\dfrac{13}{42}=3\dfrac{3}{42}$ not $\dfrac{2}{13}$'
		Substitutes into $\dfrac{2}{t+w}$ and justifies why this must be incorrect eg ■ '$\dfrac{1}{2}+\dfrac{1}{3}=\dfrac{2}{5}$ not big enough.' ■ '$\dfrac{1}{3}+\dfrac{1}{3}=\dfrac{2}{6}=\dfrac{1}{3}$ but $2\times\dfrac{1}{3}\neq\dfrac{1}{3}$'	
		Substitutes into all of $\dfrac{1}{t}+\dfrac{1}{w}=\dfrac{2}{t+w}$ and shows that the LHS ≠ RHS eg ■ '$\dfrac{1}{2}+\dfrac{1}{4}=\dfrac{2}{2+4}$ $\dfrac{3}{4}\neq\dfrac{2}{6}$'	Accept implicit indication that the LHS ≠ RHS eg '$\dfrac{1}{0.5}+\dfrac{1}{0.5}=\dfrac{2}{0.5+0.5}$ $2+2=\dfrac{2}{1}$ $4=2$'
		Correctly adds their chosen fractions and justifies why this $\neq\dfrac{2}{t+w}$ eg ■ '$\dfrac{1}{2}+\dfrac{1}{3}=\dfrac{5}{6}$ which can't be written in fifths.'	

Marks	Question 21 (cont)	Numbers (cont)
	Correct response	**Additional guidance**
	For 2m (cont) <u>Use of algebra:</u> The most common types of response are shown below. Gives the correct algebraic addition of $\frac{1}{t} + \frac{1}{w}$ eg ■ 'It should be $(t + w) \div tw$' Manipulates $\frac{1}{t} + \frac{1}{w} = \frac{2}{t + w}$ to show it cannot be correct eg ■ '$\frac{t + w}{t} + \frac{t + w}{w} = 2$ $w(t + w) + t(t + w) = 2tw$ $(t + w)^2 = 2tw$ but $(t + w)^2 = t^2 + w^2 + 2tw$' **For only 1m** chooses values for t and w **and** correctly adds the fractions, giving the answer as a fraction or decimal.	For 2m or 1m **do not accept** only a description of the algebra or a description of the process of adding fractions eg '1 is divided by t and 1 by w, not by $t + w$.' 'You have to get a common denominator.' **For 1m** ignore incorrect processing after correct substitution and addition.

Mark Scheme Paper 1

Marks		Question 22	Supermarket
		Correct response	**Additional guidance**
1m	a	Indicates, as a probability, a value between 0.78 and 0.8(0) inclusive, provided there is no evidence that other than 100 customers have been used eg ■ ' $\frac{80}{100}$ ' ■ ' $\frac{4}{5}$ '	**Do not accept** other than 100 customers used eg accept ' $\frac{78}{100}$ ' but not ' $\frac{78}{99}$ '
1m	b	Indicates, as a probability, a value between 0.6(0) and 0.68 inclusive eg ■ ' $\frac{60}{100}$ '	This probability should also be based on 100 customers. However, if it is clear that the only error in (a) and (b) is using consistent but incorrect number of customers, this mark may be awarded eg ' $\frac{80}{98}$ ' given in (a), accept ' $\frac{60}{98}$ ' in (b)
1m	c	**For 1m** shows in working the total for *fx* is 274	
1m		**For 1m** correctly evaluates their total for *fx* ÷ 100 eg ■ for a total *fx* of 274, '2.74'	Accept their total for *fx* ÷ 100 rounded or truncated, provided it is not one of the numbers printed anywhere in the table. If it is one of these numbers, the correct method of ÷ 100, or a more accurate value must be seen in the working. Similarly, only accept a range such as '2 - 3 mins' if correct working or a correct value is seen. If no incorrect working is shown, accept 2.7 or 2.74 for 2m. Accept a correct conversion to minutes and seconds, eg for 2.74 accept a value between 2 mins 44 and 2 mins 45 inclusive, or any equivalent such as $2\frac{3}{4}$ minutes. **Do not accept** an incorrect conversion eg, for 2.74 '3 mins 14 secs' '3.14 mins' '3 to 4 mins'

Mark Scheme Paper 1

Marks		Question 22 (cont)	Supermarket (cont)
		Correct response	**Additional guidance**

1m	d	Gives a valid different way.
		Possible ways include:
		
		Using different times of the day
		eg
		■ 'Survey in the morning and in the afternoon.'
		■ 'Do it for a longer time.'
		■ 'Use a quiet time and a rush hour.'
		■ 'Do it at midday when it's busiest.'
		
		Using different days
		eg
		■ 'Do it on a weekday and a weekend.'
		■ 'Try Thursday and Friday.'
		
		Surveying more of the existing checkouts
		eg
		■ 'Do more checkouts.'
		■ 'Look at other checkouts to see how fast they go.'
		■ 'Record for trolley queues and basket queues.'
		■ 'Use more tills.'
		
		Recording the waiting times to a greater degree of accuracy
		eg
		■ 'Use exact times.'
		■ 'Be more accurate on the times.'
		■ 'Use a stop watch.'
		■ 'Decrease the time intervals.'
		■ 'Put some decimal places in the readings.'
		■ 'Record as 0-, 0.5-, 1-, 1.5, and so on.'
		
		Asking customers' opinions
		eg
		■ 'Give the customers a sheet to fill out.'
		■ 'Find out if other customers are unhappy.'
		
		Obtaining more detailed information
		eg
		■ 'Record how many people are waiting before the customer.'
		■ 'See how long the queue is.'
		■ 'Record how many items each person has.'
		■ 'See if older people take longer.'
		
		Comparing with other shops
		eg
		■ 'Time other supermarkets.'
			Ignore unacceptable responses given alongside a correct response
			eg, accept
			  'Draw a pie chart and do some different checkouts.'
			
			Do not accept responses which imply more customers should be asked; this information is given.
			
			Do not accept responses which give a remedy rather than further information
			eg
			  'Use bar-code readers.'
			  'Employ different people.'
			  'Open more checkouts.'
			
			Do not accept responses which imply the graph should change or that the graph determines the waiting times
			eg
			  'Add more time on the scale.'
			  'Put more categories after the 5 minutes.'
			
			Do not accept responses which simply change the presentation of data
			eg
			  'Use a pie chart.'
			  'Use percentages.'
			
			Do not accept responses which imply a statistical analysis on the existing data
			eg
			  'Use the mode.'
			  'Find the mean.'

29

Mark Scheme Paper 1

Marks		Question 23	Algebra
		Correct response	**Additional guidance**
1m	a	Indicates 1500	
1m		Indicates 20	
1m	b	Indicates a correct, fully simplified expression eg • '$\frac{3d}{5}$' • '$\frac{3}{5}d$' • '$3d \div 5$' • '$0.6d$'	**Do not accept** unconventional fractions eg '$\frac{1.5}{2.5}d$'
1m	c	Indicates a correct, fully simplified expression for $3(x-2) - 2(4-3x)$ eg • '$9x - 14$' • '$-14 + 9 \times x$'	
1m		Indicates a correct simplified expression for $(x+2)(x+3)$ eg • '$x^2 + 5x + 6$' • '$x^2 + 6 + 5 \times x$'	x^2 should be written with index notation, ie not as $x \times x$ or xx. However, do not penalise this error more than once within the question. ***Throughout the question* do not accept** continuation from a correct response to an incorrect response eg '$x^2 + 5x + 6 = 5x^3 + 6$'
1m		Indicates a correct simplified expression for $(x+4)(x-1)$ eg • '$x^2 + 3x - 4$' • '$3 \times x - 4 + x^2$'	
1m		Indicates a correct simplified expression for $(x-2)^2$ eg • '$x^2 - 4x + 4$' • '$x^2 + x \times -4 + 4$' • '$x^2 + 4(-x + 1)$'	

Mark Scheme Paper 1

Marks		Question 24	Graphs
		Correct response	**Additional guidance**
1m	a	Draws a parabola inside the given curve, passing within 2mm of (0,0).	Accept a parabola which is not accurate provided the pupil's intention is clear. Accept a parabola which touches the given curve initially eg **Do not accept** a parabola which touches the given curve at a later stage eg **Do not accept** a parabola drawn as straight lines.
1m	b	Indicates a correct equation eg ■ '$y = -x^2$' ■ '$-y = x^2$'	Accept correct but unconventional equations eg '$y = \dfrac{x^2}{-1}$'
1m	c	Indicates a correct equation eg ■ '$y = x^2 + 1$' ■ '$y - 1 = x^2$'	If both equations have been written as expressions in terms of x but are otherwise correct, allow the mark for part (c) only eg award 0 in (b), 1 in (c) for '$-x^2$, $x^2 + 1$' similarly for 'A $= -x^2$, B $= x^2 + 1$'
1m	d	For **2m** indicates the two correct inequalities eg ■ For only **1m** indicates one correct and no incorrect. **or** Indicates one or both correct with only one non-conflicting incorrect, as detailed in the additional guidance.	Accept any indication of the correct inequalities. $y < 2$ conflicts with $y > 2$ $y > x^2$ conflicts with $y < x^2$

Mark Scheme Paper 1

Marks		Question 25	Values
		Correct response	**Additional guidance**
1m	a	Indicates the **top** statement **and** gives a correct explanation eg ■ '4 × 10³ = 4000, 4³ = 64' ■ '4 × 10³ means 4 × 10 × 10 × 10 which is greater than 4 × 4 × 4' ■ 'Just the 10³ on its own is more than 4³'	Accept any indication that $4 \times 10^3 > 4^3$, even if no statement is ticked. Provided the top statement is indicated, accept evaluation of 4×10^3 or 10^3 as sufficient eg '4 × 10³ = 4000' '10³ means × 1000' **Do not accept** an incorrect statement ticked, even if the explanation is correct. The explanation need not compute values for 4×10^3 or 4^3. However, any computation must be correct hence **do not accept** incorrect computations eg '4³ = 16² = 256'
1m	b	Indicates the **last** statement, ie 0.36×10^5	
1m	c	Indicates the **first** statement, ie 25×10^{-4}	
1m	d	Indicates a correct simplified response eg ■ '6' ■ '6 × 10⁰'	The question does not ask for a response in standard form, hence accept a correct number × 10 to the appropriate power eg, for the second part '300 × 10²'
1m		Indicates a correct simplified response eg ■ '3 × 10⁴' ■ '30000'	Accept a correct value written as a fraction with the denominator 1, otherwise **do not accept** partial simplification eg, for the second part $\frac{6 \times 10^4}{2}$

Marks		Question 26	Languages
		Correct response	**Additional guidance**
1m	a	Indicates a correct probability eg ■ $\frac{69}{100}$	
1m	b	Indicates a correct probability eg ■ $\frac{27}{57}$	Accept decimals or percentages which round to 0.47 or 47%
1m	c	Indicates the correct calculation eg ■ · · · · · · · · · · · · $\boxed{\frac{27}{100} \times \frac{26}{99}}$ · · · ·	Accept any indication.

Marks		Question 27	Shape
		Correct response	**Additional guidance**
3m	a	**For 3m** gives a complete justification showing a correct expansion of $(3a)^2$ to $9a^2$, **and** that the area is found by adding the area of the first 2 semi-circles and subtracting the area of the 3rd eg • 'Big semi-circle is $\frac{9\pi a^2}{2}$, medium $\frac{4\pi a^2}{2}$, little $\frac{\pi a^2}{2}$. Big + medium – little = $\frac{12\pi a^2}{2}$ ' • '$9\pi a^2 + 4\pi a^2 - \pi a^2 = 12\pi a^2$ but it's semi-circles so it's half of that.' • '$4.5 \times \pi a^2 + 2 \times \pi a^2 - 0.5 \times \pi a^2$' • '$\frac{1}{2}\pi a^2 (9 + 4 - 1)$'	*Throughout the question* do **not accept** sight of $6\pi a^2$ as justification; this has been given. For 3m **do not accept** subsequent incorrect working. For 3m **do not accept** a numerical substitution for π. For 3m or 2m **do not accept** expressions with brackets as evidence. The expressions must be multiplied out.
		For only 2m shows a correct expansion to find the areas of all 3 semi-circles (or circles), even if there are other errors eg • '$9\pi a^2 + 4\pi a^2 + \pi a^2$' • $\frac{9\pi a^2 + 4\pi a^2 + \pi a^2}{2}$	**For 2m or 1m** accept a numerical substitution for π.
		For only 1m shows the correct expansion of $(3a)^2$ to $9a^2$ **or** Shows a correct method with the only error being that $(3a)^2$ is incorrectly expanded eg • '$6\pi a^2 + 4\pi a^2 - \pi a^2 = 9\pi a^2$ then $\div 2$' **or** Shows a correct starting point with correct values substituted eg • '$\frac{1}{2}[\pi \times (3a)^2 + \pi \times (2a)^2 - \pi \times a^2]$'	**Do not accept** incorrect algebra as a correct starting point eg '$\frac{1}{2}[\pi \times 3a^2 + \pi \times 2a^2 - \pi \times a^2]$'

Marks		Question 27 (cont)	Shape (cont)
		Correct response	**Additional guidance**
2m	b	For **2m** indicates a correct equation with the simplification of $12 \div 6$ to 2 eg ■ '$a = \sqrt{\dfrac{2}{\pi}}$' ■ '$a = \dfrac{\sqrt{2}}{\sqrt{\pi}}$' ■ '$a = \sqrt{2} \div \sqrt{\pi}$' For only **1m** gives an otherwise correct expression but with a numerical substitution for π eg ■ '$\sqrt{\dfrac{2}{3.14}}$' **or** Shows correct working with only one error, or one omitted simplification, ie shows any of: $a = \sqrt{\dfrac{12}{6\pi}}$, $a^2 = \dfrac{2}{\pi}$, $a = \sqrt{(2\pi)}$	For **2m do not accept** a numerical substitution for π. For **2m do not accept** subsequent incorrect working. For **2m or 1m** ignore correct units given in the equation eg, for **2m** '$\sqrt{\dfrac{2cm^2}{\pi}}$' For **1m** accept a numerical substitution for π. For **1m** accept subsequent incorrect working. For **1m** ignore incorrect units given.

[Blank page]

Marks		Question 1	Sponsors
		Correct response	**Additional guidance**
2m	a	For **2m** completes the table correctly eg ■ Ben 20p Cal **25p** **Jan** 30p **Kim** 15p **Wyn** 20p For only **1m** completes three out of the four entries correctly.	**Do not accept** failure to specify the units eg '25'
1m	b	Indicates £1.10	**Allow follow through** from part (a) provided an entry has been made for Cal in the 'Amount for each length' column.
1m	c	Indicates £20.25	
1m	d	Indicates £18	
1m		Indicates £4.50	**Allow follow through** from an incorrect total, rounded or truncated to a whole number of pence eg for £1800 given as the total, accept £450

Marks		Question 2	Yen
1m	a	Indicates 240	*Throughout the question,* ignore decimal points or indications of the thousands digit eg '2.40' '2,513' '3:052'
1m	b	Indicates 302	
1m	c	Indicates 2513	
1m	d	Indicates 3052	

Marks		Question 3	Balancing
		Correct response	**Additional guidance**
1m	a	Indicates 4	*Throughout the question*, accept any indication of the correct response, provided the pupil's intention is clear eg Correct objects drawn.
1m	b	Indicates 5	
1m	c	Indicates 6	*Throughout the question*, ignore objects drawn if numbers are given.

1m	d	Correctly indicates the bottle on one side, and the boxes and can on the other
		eg
		
		  ■
		
		  ■ boxes bottle
		
		  ■ 'box, box, can = bottle'
		  ■ 'bottle = the rest'
			Do not accept extra objects drawn or indicated.
			
			Do not accept responses which refer to only one box
			eg
			    'box, can = bottle'

Mark Scheme Paper 2

Marks		Question 4	Calendar
		Correct response	**Additional guidance**

1m	a	Indicates 18(th).	Accept correct month and correct or incorrect year
			eg
			    '18 Jan'
			    '1.18.99'

1m 1m	b	Indicates 4 Indicates 5	

1m	c	Completes the sentence correctly, indicating that there are
		    more **than**
		    Wednesdays **or** Sundays
		    Thursdays Mondays
		                      Tuesdays
		                      Fridays **or**
		                      Saturdays	

1m	d	Indicates February 11
		eg
		  ■ 'Feb 11th'
		  ■ '2/11'
			Accept correct or incorrect year or day of the week
			eg
			    '11 2 97'
			    'Tues, 11 Feb'
			
			Do not accept responses which do not indicate both the date and the month.

1m	e	Indicates 3	Accept responses indicating one day less
			eg
			    '2 weeks and 6 days.'
			
			Do not accept the answer given only in days
			eg
			    '21 days'

1m	f	Indicates Saturday.	Accept any indication eg '7, 14, 21, 28' Ignore further multiples of 7 **Do not accept** fewer than the first four dates.

Mark Scheme Paper 2

Marks		Question 5	Patterns
		Correct response	**Additional guidance**
1m	a	Indicates 4 eg <li> '4' <li> 'He adds one tile on each corner.' <li> Diagram drawn showing that a tile is added to each corner.	**Do not accept** the total numbers of tiles in each pattern eg '4, 8, 12'
1m	b	Indicates 24	
1m	c	Indicates 36	
1m	d	Indicates 10	

Marks		Question 6	Spinners
		Correct response	**Additional guidance**
1m	a	Indicates S.	*Throughout the question,* drawing and shading need not be accurate provided the pupil's intention is clear.
1m	b	Indicates R.	
1m	c	Shades the whole spinner.	

1m	d	Shades half the spinner, using a diameter or radii to distinguish the sectors
		eg
		
			Accept any surface for the area which is not shaded
			eg
			    plain
			    striped
			    coloured
			
			Do not accept shading in which there is no intention to divide the surface into sectors
			eg

Mark Scheme Paper 2

Marks		Question 7	Games
		Correct response	**Additional guidance**
1m	a	Indicates Liz.	Accept the name written in the table.
1m	b	Indicates Jim.	
1m	c	Gives a valid advantage of Meg's table. This may relate to: The ready availability of summary information eg ■ 'You can see who won overall.' ■ 'It tells you how many games each person won.' ■ 'Meg's way is much better because it's easy to see each person's total.' ■ 'You can see who won the most.' ■ 'Everything is all in one table.' ■ 'You don't have to count names.' ■ 'It gives you a running total all the way through the competition.' ■ 'It's easy to keep count.' ■ 'You can see who is winning.' ■ 'It is less confusing.' ■ 'It's easier to count the tallies.' Ease of recording eg ■ 'It's quick to fill in.' ■ 'You just have to put lines.' ■ 'You can count in fives.' ■ 'It takes up less space.'	Accept a correct response which is accompanied by an irrelevant reason or a reason which applies to both. **Do not accept** responses which simply state that one or the other method is better eg 'Jim's way is much better.' 'Tally charts are better.' **Do not accept** vague responses which could apply equally well to either record eg 'You can see the total number of games they played.' 'This chart is easy to use.' **Do not accept** false statements, even if they are accompanied by a valid advantage eg 'Meg's way is quick to fill in and *it tells you who won each game.*' 'Jim's table *shows the order in which the games were played* and how often they won.'
1m	d	Gives a valid advantage of Jim's table. This may relate to: The detail of the information eg ■ 'You can see who won each game.' ■ 'You can tell who won the Ludo.' ■ 'You know what games each person won.' ■ 'You can see who won what.' ■ 'It tells how many of each game each person won.' ■ 'Jim's way is more detailed.' ■ 'It shows in what order people won.' Security/Accuracy eg ■ 'You can't cheat with Jim's way.' ■ 'You are less likely to make mistakes.'	**Do not accept** a description of the method used with no indication of its advantages eg 'Meg's is good because she uses a tally chart.' 'Jim gives all the names.' 'Jim sorted the results out into columns.' 'Jim did each game separately.'

Marks		Question 8	Rivers
		Correct response	**Additional guidance**

1m	a	Completes the column of lengths to the nearest 100 correctly
		eg
		■ '400
		     300
		     300
		     200
		     100'	

1m		Indicates Thames **and** Trent.	Accept rivers in either order.

1m	b	Completes the column of lengths to the nearest 10 correctly
		eg
		■ '350
		     350
		     300
		     220
		     110'
			Allow follow through from an incorrect table **provided** all the numbers in the table are of three digits.
			
			Accept 215 rounded down to 210.
			
			Accept any unambiguous indication of the correct rivers
			eg
			    '297' for Trent and '346' for Thames.
			    '350' for Severn and Thames.

1m	a	Indicates Severn **and** Thames.	

Marks		Question 8 (cont)	Rivers (cont)
		Correct response	**Additional guidance**
1m	c	Indicates a number greater than or equal to 150 and less than or equal to 155 ($150 \le n \le 155$) eg ■ '150' ■ '151' ■ '152' ■ '153' ■ '154' ■ '155'	
2m	d	**For 2m** indicates one whole number greater than or equal to 245 and less than or equal to 250 ($245 \le n \le 250$) eg ■ '245' ■ '246' ■ '247' ■ '248' ■ '249' ■ '250' **and** indicates one **different** whole number greater than or equal to 250 and less than or equal to 255 ($250 \le n \le 255$) eg ■ '250' ■ '251' ■ '252' ■ '253' ■ '254' ■ '255' **For only 1m** indicates one correct number but with the other number missing or incorrect eg ■ '253' and '252' ■ '250' and '250' ■ '245' ■ '247' and '252.5' **or** Indicates two different whole numbers which have the same value to the nearest 10 (but not 250), but are different to the nearest 100 eg ■ '146' and '153' **or** Indicates two numbers which fit the criteria but are not both whole numbers eg ■ '249.999...' and '250.1'	Accept numbers in either order. **For 2m do not accept** 250 indicated twice.

Mark Scheme Paper 2

Marks		Question 9	Triangle
		Correct response	**Additional guidance**
1m	a	Draws another triangle to form a 2 by 3 rectangle eg 	*Throughout the question*, drawings need not be accurate provided the pupil's intention to draw a congruent triangle in the correct position is clear. **Do not accept** responses to part (a) given in part (b), or responses to part (b) given in part (a).
1m	b	Draws another congruent triangle to form a bigger triangle eg 	
1m	c	Draws another congruent triangle to form the other bigger triangle.	

Marks		Question 10	Paint
		Correct response	**Additional guidance**
2m	a	**For 2m** indicates 6 red **and** 14 blue. **For only 1m** indicates one correct value in the correct position. **or** Indicates both values, but in the wrong order. **or** Indicates another pair of numbers, other than 3 and 7, which are in the ratio 3 to 7 eg ■ '30' and '70' ■ '60' and '140'	Accept correct answers given in other metric units, provided the units are shown eg '6000 millilitres'
2m	b	**For 2m** indicates 6.5 yellow **and** 3.5 red eg ■ '$6\frac{1}{2}$' and '$3\frac{1}{2}$' **For only 1m** indicates one correct value in the correct position. **or** Indicates both values, but in the wrong order. **or** Indicates another pair of numbers, other than 13 and 7, which are in the ratio 13 to 7 eg ■ '130' and '70' ■ '0.65' and '0.35'	

Marks		Question 11	L-triominoes
		Correct response	**Additional guidance**
1m	a	Draws a shape different from that given made with two L-triominoes with only one line of symmetry eg 	*Throughout the question* drawings need not be accurate provided the pupil's intention is clear. Accept any or no internal lines showing individual squares forming triominoes, or the triominoes themselves. *Throughout the question* ignore attempts to draw lines of symmetry. *Throughout the question* accept enlargements of acceptable responses eg, for part (a) *Throughout the question* ignore copies, rotations, reflections or enlargements of the examples given in the question given in addition to acceptable shapes. *Throughout the question* **do not accept** responses in the wrong answer spaces, unless the pupil's intentions are clear. *Throughout the question* **do not accept** shapes which are not composed of two triominoes. Accept arrangements of two triominoes which have the correct symmetries but do not touch or touch only at a vertex or vertices eg, for part (a)

Marks		Question 11	L-triominoes (cont)
		Correct response	**Additional guidance**
1m	b	Draws a shape made with two L-triominoes with two lines of symmetry eg 	Accept arrangements of two triominoes which have the correct symmetries but do not touch or touch only at a vertex or vertices eg, for part (b)
1m	c	Draws a shape different from that given made with two L-triominoes with rotational symmetry of order two eg 	eg, for part (c)
1m	d	Draws a shape made with two L-triominoes with two lines of symmetry and rotational symmetry of order two eg 	eg, for part (d)

Mark Scheme Paper 2

Marks		Question 12	Ages
		Correct response	**Additional guidance**
1m	a	Indicates a value in the range 20 to 30% inclusive.	Accept equivalent fractions or decimals written outside the answer space.
1m	b	Indicates a number in the range 2 to 3 inclusive.	Accept a correct number of people which is not given in the answer space eg '2,500,000' **Allow follow through** from a percentage given in part (a).

1m	c	Indicates that the total number of people in each country needs to be taken into account
		eg
		■ 'Greece has more people.'
		■ 'Ireland has 3.5 and Greece has 10.'
		■ 'It's out of more people.'
		■ 'Ireland has **only** 3.5 million people.'
		■ 'The total populations are not the same.'
		■ '20% of 10 is more than 25% of 3.5'
		■ '2 > 0.875'
			Accept explanations which indicate that the pie charts give only the proportions, or that they do not give the numbers of people
			eg
			    'The charts only show the percentages.'
			    'It doesn't give the actual numbers of people.'
			    'One per cent in Greece is worth more than one per cent in Ireland.'
			    'The chart for Ireland is on a bigger scale.'
			    '1% for Greece is about 3% for Ireland.'
			    'It's only the proportion of people under 15 which is greater in Ireland.'
			    'The charts are drawn to different scales.'
			    'There are 10 million people in Greece so there is a bigger pie for Greece.'
			
			Ignore irrelevant statements which accompany a valid reason
			eg
			    'The charts are not dead accurate, and there are more people in Greece.'
			
			Do not accept explanations which could relate to the size of the countries and not to the populations
			eg
			    'Ireland is smaller.'
			
			Do not accept explanations which state only one of the populations, without indicating that this is less or greater than the other
			eg
			    'Ireland has a population of 3.5 million.'
			
			Do not accept false statements
			eg
			    'There are more people in Greece so 10% would look larger on Ireland than on Greece.'
			    'The chart for Ireland is on a smaller scale.'
			    'The chart for Ireland is bigger.'

Marks		Question 12	Ages (cont)
		Correct response	**Additional guidance**
2m	d	**For 2m** draws a correct pie chart, showing sectors with 2, $3\frac{1}{2}$, $2\frac{1}{2}$ and 2 of the 10% sectors given in the question eg **For only 1m** draws a pie chart with four sectors, two of which are the correct size.	Drawings need not be accurate provided the pupil's intention is clear. **Do not accept** pie charts which have fewer than 4 or more than 4 sectors.
1m		Labels their 4-sector pie chart, with the largest of their four sectors labeled '15 - 39', the second largest labeled '40 - 59', and the remaining two labeled 'under 15' and 'over 59'.	The two smallest sectors may be taken in either order for the purpose of labeling. Accept the use of a key to indicate the age ranges covered by each sector. Accept correct percentages given in addition to age ranges, but **do not accept** percentages instead of age ranges. **Do not accept** incorrect labels eg '15' for 'under 15' **Do not accept** labels on two sectors which are the same size, unless they are smaller than the other two. **Do not accept** labels on three or four sectors which are the same size.

Marks		Question 13 Marking overlay provided	Nets
		Correct response	**Additional guidance**
1m	a	Indicates the correct net, and no other nets eg ■ 	Accept any indication.

2m	b	**For 2m** draws a semi-circle, radius 4cm ±
		2mm, and its diameter, as in the overlay.
		
		For only 1m draws a semi-circle, radius
		8cm ± 2mm, and its diameter, as in the
		overlay.
			For 2m or 1m accept more than a semi-circle
			drawn, provided at least one acceptable semi-
			circle and its diameter are drawn
			eg
			    Attempts to draw a complete net of the
			    box.
			    Draws a whole circle with a diameter.
			    Draws a part of a circle greater than a semi-
			    circle, with a diameter.

Marks		Question 14	Doubles
		Correct response	**Additional guidance**
1m	a	Indicates a correct probability eg <ul><li>' $\frac{35}{36}$ '</li><li>'0.97'</li></ul>	**Do not accept** incomplete processing eg $\quad$ '1 $-\frac{1}{36}$ '
1m	b	Ticks the ' $\frac{1}{36}$ ' box **and** correctly justifies why the probability is $\frac{1}{36}$ eg <ul><li>'It's $\frac{1}{6} \times \frac{1}{6}$ '</li><li>'It's a 1 in 36 chance.'</li></ul>**or** Explains it is the same as for the previous throw eg <ul><li>'What you throw doesn't affect what you throw the next time.'</li><li>'It doesn't change.'</li><li>'A double is as likely to appear again.'</li><li>'It's still 1 in 36'</li><li>'Because it is fair.'</li><li>'The odds are the same.'</li><li>'The throws are independent.'</li><li>'They're still the same dice.'</li></ul>	Accept any indication provided it is clear the probability is still $\frac{1}{36}$ **Do not accept** the word 'even' to mean equal eg $\quad$ 'There are even chances of getting double 6 on each throw.'
1m	c	Indicates a correct probability eg <ul><li>' $\frac{1}{36}$ '</li></ul>	Accept decimals or percentages rounded or truncated to 2 or more s.f. eg $\quad$ '0.02777' Accept a reference to earlier in the question eg $\quad$ 'Same as double 6'
1m	d	Indicates a correct probability eg <ul><li>' $\frac{6}{36}$ '</li><li>' $\frac{1}{6}$ '</li></ul>	Accept decimals or percentages rounded or truncated to 2 or more s.f. eg $\quad$ '0.166' **Do not accept** incomplete processing eg $\quad$ ' $\frac{1}{36} \times 6$ '

Mark Scheme Paper 2

Marks		Question 15	Continents
		Correct response	**Additional guidance**

1m	a	Indicates South America.	Accept any indication of the continent or of the calculation correctly evaluated
			eg
			    '17793'
			    '17802.6'
			    '11.99'
			
			Do not accept an ambiguous response
			eg
			    'America.'

2m	b	**For 2m** indicates 9 or 8.9(...) eg ■ '8.9' **For only 1m** shows a correct method eg ■ '13209 ÷ 148355' ■ '100 ÷ 148355 × 13209'	**For 1m** allow a misread which has been correctly evaluated, provided it is clear which data have been used eg '44250 ÷ 148355 = 29.8%'
2m	c	**For 2m** indicates 500 **or** Indicates a value between 489 and 499 **and** shows a correct method eg ■ '148355 × 10 ÷ 3' ■ '150 × 3.3' **For only 1m** shows a correct method eg ■ '÷ 30 then × 100' ■ '× 10 ÷ 3' ■ '÷ 0.3' ■ '× 3.3' ■ '500 000 000' on the answer line. **or** Shows a correct value for the amount of water eg ■ '350' ■ '350 000 000' not on the answer line.	**For 2m** accept 500 000 000, or other correct indication of km^2, **provided** it is not written on the answer line. **For 2m** as the question asks for an approximation accept 3.3, or better, for $3\frac{1}{3}$ **For 1m** accept 3 as an approximation for $3\frac{1}{3}$ **For 1m** accept a misread of the question, whereby a pupil takes 150 to be 70%, and continues to an answer of 214.(...) million km^2.

Mark Scheme Paper 2

Marks		Question 16	Drawing
		Correct response	**Additional guidance**
2m		**For 2m** draws the correct shape in the correct orientation eg 	**For 2m** either all lines showing small cubes should be shown individually, or the complete outline only should be given. Hence, **do not accept** inconsistent use of lines eg
		For only 1m draws the correct outline shape in the correct orientation but adds or omits lines eg 	**For 2m or 1m** the drawing need not be correctly aligned with the drawings in the question.
		or Makes an isometric drawing to show the L-shape from a different view from any shown in the question eg 	For L-shapes from different views **do not accept** inconsistent use of lines eg
		or Draws an otherwise correct shape that is 2 or 4 cubes high eg 	For otherwise correct shapes that are 2 or 4 cubes high **do not accept** inconsistent use of lines.

[Blank page]

Mark Scheme Paper 2

Marks		Question 17	Scores
		Correct response	**Additional guidance**
2m	a	**For 2m** indicates 65 **For only 1m** shows the value 180 (or 60 × 3) eg ■ '60 × 3 - (62 + 53)' ■ '180 – 115' ■ '62 + 53 + ? = 180' **or** Shows a correct method with not more than one computational error eg ■ '62 is 2 above the mean, 53 is 7 below so C is 5 above.' ■ '62 + 53 = 115, 115 ÷ 3 = 38 60 – 38 = 22, 22 × 3 = 66' ■ '$\frac{62 + 53 + x}{3} = 60$'	**For 2m** accept indication that 65 is a minimum score eg '65 or more' **For 2m** accept 65 embedded but with no value indicated on the answer line eg '62 + 53 + 65 = 180, 180 ÷ 3 = 60' However, if 65 is embedded and a different value is indicated on the answer line, award only **1m**.
1m	b	Indicates, in any order, 30 and 50	
1m	c	Indicates positive relationship eg ■ A & B ☐☐☐✓☐	Accept any indication.
1m		Indicates no relationship eg ■ A & C ☐☐✓☐☐	
1m	d	**Follows through** correctly from responses given in part (c) eg, for 2m awarded in (c) ■ A & B ☐☐☐✓☐ 1m A & C ☐☐✓☐☐ 1m B & C ☐☐☐✓☐ 1m	In each case where follow through is allowed, the category for B & C is the same as for A & C. **Follow through** should **only** apply from responses in (c) which show some understanding, ie those shown below: one of ┌ or ┐ or ┐ A & B ✓✓☐☐✓ 0m A & C ☐☐✓☐☐ 1m B & C ☐☐✓☐☐ 1m A & B ☐☐☐✓☐ 1m A & C ☐✓☐☐☐ 0m B & C ☐✓☐☐☐ 1m A & B ☐☐☐☐✓ 0m A & C ☐☐✓☐☐ 0m B & C ☐☐☐✓☐ 1m

Marks		Question 18	Coffee
		Correct response	**Additional guidance**
2m	a	**For 2m** indicates 60	Possible methods include:
			Area of given triangle × 6
		For only 1m shows a complete and correct method with not more than one computational error eg ■ '5 × 4 ÷ 2 = 20, 20 × 6 = 120' ■ '$\frac{1}{2}$ of 5 is 1.5, 4 × 1.5 ÷ 2 = 3, 80 – (3 × 4) = 68' ■ 'It's $\frac{3}{4}$ of the rectangle and $\frac{3}{4}$ of 80 = 65'	eg '(4 × 5) ÷ 2 × 6' Area of rectangle – area of 4 corner triangles eg '10 × 8 – (4 × 2.5 ÷ 2) × 4' 'Rectangle = 80 - 20 for all triangles.'
		or Shows a complete method, including evaluation of the final answer, with no computational errors and not more than one conceptual error eg ■ 'One triangle is 4 × 5 = 20, 20 × 6 = 120' ■ '4 × 2.5 = 10, 10 × 4 = 40, 80 – 40 = 40'	Area of rectangle × $\frac{3}{4}$ Area of parallelogram formed by the triangles eg '5 × 12' '15 × 4' Areas of rectangles formed by rearrangement eg
		or Correctly finds the area of either of the triangles, showing a valid method ■ '4 × 5 ÷ 2 = 10' ■ '4 × 2.5 ÷ 2 = 5'	'40 + 20' Area of trapezium × 2 eg '(10 + 5) ÷ 2 × 4 × 2'
			10 and 5 are also values shown in the question, hence **do not accept** these as areas without a valid method.

Marks		Question 18 (cont)	Coffee (cont)
		Correct response	**Additional guidance**
3m	b	**For 3m follows through** correctly to find the correct number of grams for their area eg ■ '240' for the correct response of '60' in part (a). ■ Their (a) × 4 correctly evaluated. **For only 2m** uses their area and shows all 3 steps even if there are computational errors. **or** Uses their area and correctly calculates any 2 of the 3 steps required, even if the other step is incorrect or omitted. **For only 1m** uses their area and correctly calculates any 1 of the steps, even if the other steps are incorrect or omitted. **or** Calculates 80% of the length and converts to grams, without using their area eg ■ '4'	Only allow '240' from an incorrect response from part (a) if there is evidence of successful re-calculation of the area. The 3 steps, which may be done in any order, are: ① × 10 to find the volume, ② a correct method for finding 80% of a number, ③ ÷ 2 to convert to grams. **For 2m** if one step is omitted, follow through as shown below will apply: | steps	follow through correctly evaluated	(a) correct as 60
---	---	---
① and ②	(a) × 8	480
① and ③	(a) × 5	300
② and ③	(a) × 0.4	24 | **For 1m** if two steps are omitted, follow through as shown below will apply: | step	follow through correctly evaluated	(a) correct as 60
---	---	---
①	(a) × 10	600
②	(a) × 0.8	48
③	(a) ÷ 2	30	
2m	c	**For 2m** indicates a value between £0.96 and £0.97 inclusive. **For only 1m** shows a correct method, in pounds or pence ■ '219 ÷ 227' ■ '2.19 ÷ 227' ■ '227 ÷ 100 = 2.27, 2.19 ÷ 2.27' ■ '96.47p' on the answer line. ■ '97' on the answer line. ■ The digits 9647... seen.	

Mark Scheme Paper 2

Marks		Question 19	Table
		Correct response	**Additional guidance**

| 3m | a | **For 3m** justifies through a correct calculation and correct interpretation that the table is not large enough. Most justifications involve calculation of the **circumference as 17m**, or **17.2 to 17.3m** inclusive, then one of: | Interpretation may either be through an explanation or by showing correct units, such as cm, m or people. |

Circumference ÷ 50 to find the space each person has, ie **34 to 35cm** inclusive
eg
- '1727 ÷ 50 = 34 No.'
- '1727 ÷ 50 = 34cm'
- 'Each person gets 0.35m'
- '5.5 ÷ 50 × 3.14 = 0.3454, Not enough.'

Circumference ÷ (0.)45 to find the number of people, ie **37 to 39** inclusive
eg
- '17.3 ÷ 0.45 = 38.4 No.'
- '38 so no.'
- '38 people could.'
- '1728 ÷ 45 < 50'

Comparing **circumference** with **50 × (0.)45**, the amount of space 50 people need
eg
- 'C = 17m, need 22.5m.'
- '50 × 45 = 2250, $2\pi r$ = 17.258 Too small.'
- '50 × 45 = 2250cm, $2\pi r$ = 17m'
- '45 × 50 > π × 550'

For only 2m makes only one error
eg
- '1727 ÷ 50 = 34 *people*.'
- '2 × 3.14 × 2.25 = 14.13, ÷ 50 = 28 No.'
- '172 ÷ 45 = 3.8 people.'
- 'Circum = 1727cm, 45 × 50 = 27250cm'

For only 1m makes only two errors
eg
- '$2\pi2.25$ = 14.1, ÷ 50 = 0.282m   *282cm*'
- '2 × π × 5.5 = 34.5, 50 × 45 = 2250'
or
Shows a correct calculation for the circumference of the table
eg
- '3.14 × 5.5'
- '17.2'
or
Uses the area formula but makes no other errors
eg
- 'π × 2.75^2 = 23.76, ÷ 50 = 47.5 Yes.'
- '23.8 ÷ 45 = 53 people.'
- '23.7m > 22.5m'

Additional guidance column:

Accept comparisons with one measurement in metres and the other in centimetres.

Accept alternative correct justifications, such as comparing the given diameter with the required diameter to seat all 50 people
eg
  '50 × 45 ÷ π > 5.5m.'

For 3m a correct value must be evaluated or explicitly compared to a given value
eg, accept
  '1727 ÷ 50 < 45'
but not
  '1727 ÷ 50 No.'

For 2m **do not accept** the use of the area formula.

Errors are defined as follows:
  Using incorrect radius, eg 2.25
  Using diameter as radius.
  Calculation not evaluated or compared.
  Incorrect conversion between units.
  Selecting wrong units.
  Making an arithmetic error.
  Interpreting incorrectly.
  Not interpreting.

Mark Scheme Paper 2

Marks		Question 19 (cont)	Table (cont)
		Correct response	**Additional guidance**
3m	b	For **3m** indicates a value between 18.84 and 18.86 inclusive. **or** Indicates 6π or 18.8 or 18.9 or 19	For **3m** accept 18 only if a correct method, or a correct response, is seen in the working. For **3m** accept correct conversion to other units, provided the units are stated eg '189000cm^2'

		For **only 2m** shows a correct evaluation of both $\pi \times 2.75^2$ and $\pi \times 1.25^2$, even if rounded or truncated
		eg
		▪ '23.7, 4.9' seen in working.
		or
		Shows a complete correct method with correct values substituted, even if incorrectly calculated
		eg
		▪ '$\pi \times 2.75^2 - \pi \times 1.25^2$'
		▪ '$\pi 2.75^2 - \pi 1.25^2 = 74.6 - 15.4 = 59.2$'
		▪ '$\pi \times 2.75^2 - \pi \times (2.75 - 1.5)^2$'
		▪ '7.5625 − 1.5625 then × 3.14'
		▪ '$(2.75 + 1.25)(2.75 - 1.25) \times \pi$'
			For **2m or 1m** accept working in other units, even if the units are not stated.
			
			For **2m do not accept** the area formula shown incorrectly
			eg
			  '$2.75\pi^2$'
			  '$(2.75 \times \pi)^2$'
			  '$2\pi \times 2.75^2$'

		For **only 1m** shows or implies that the radius of the smaller circle is 1.25 eg ▪ '1.25' shown in working, even if an incorrect formula is used. ▪ '$\pi \times (2.75 - 1.5)^2$' ▪ Area of smaller circle shown as a value between 4.84 and 4.91 inclusive. ▪ '$(\pi \times 2.75)^2 - (\pi \times 1.25)^2$ ▪ '$2 \times \pi \times 1.25$' ▪ '$\pi \times 2.5$' **or** Shows that the area of the larger circle is 24 or a value between 23.7 and 23.8 inclusive.	

Marks		Question 20	Throw
		Correct response	**Additional guidance**

1m	a	Indicates Sue **and** gives a correct explanation referring to the total number of throws
		eg
		■ 'She did it for longer.'
		■ 'The more throws, the clearer it becomes.'
		■ 'She did most.'
		■ 'She had more data.'
		■ 'The more goes you take, the more you smooth the oddities.'
			Accept any indication
			eg
			    '140'
			
			Accept explanations which imply the total number of throws is highest
			eg
			    'She did it 140 times.'
			
			Do not accept partial or incorrect explanations
			eg
			    'She has the most in 2 categories.'
			    'She has the most in each category.'

1m	b	Indicates a correct probability eg ■ $\dfrac{171}{300}$ ■ '0.57' ■ '57%'	As the question asks for an estimate, also accept $\dfrac{170}{300}$ or equivalent probability. **Do not accept** attempts to deal with sets of 3 throws eg $\dfrac{171}{300} \times 3$

2m	c	**For 2m** gives 3 correct values that sum to 300
		eg
		■ '$166\dfrac{2}{3}$, 125, $8\dfrac{1}{3}$'
		
		For only 1m indicates any 2 correct values.
			For 2m the values must sum to 300
			
			For 2m or 1m accept correct values that have been rounded or truncated to the nearest integer, or to 1 or more d.p.
			eg, for 2m
			    '166, 125, 9'
			    '167, 125, 8'
			    '166.7, 125, 8.3'
			eg, for 1m
			    '166, 125, 8'
			
			For 2m or 1m accept correct values expressed as a proportion of 300
			eg, for 2m
			    $\dfrac{167}{300}, \dfrac{125}{300}, \dfrac{8}{300}$
			
			For 1m accept correct percentages provided they sum to 100
			eg
			    '56%, 42%, 2%'
			    '56%, 41%, 3%'
			    '55%, 42%, 3%'
			For 1m also accept correct percentages rounded to the nearest integer
			eg
			    '56%, 42%, 3%'

Mark Scheme Paper 2

Marks		Question 20 (cont)	Throw (cont)
		Correct response	**Additional guidance**
1m	d	Indicates the number of throws needs increasing eg ■ 'Do it more times to get closer.' ■ 'More throws needed.' or Indicates results cannot be predicted exactly eg ■ 'It's just chance.' ■ 'Freak results happen.' ■ 'You won't always throw what you want.' ■ 'It's random.' ■ 'Nothing is certain.' ■ 'For every throw it could be all different.' ■ 'The numbers could be very different.' ■ 'It only shows you what to expect.'	Ignore other information given alongside a correct response eg 'Nothing is certain and the pupils didn't throw them the same amount of times.' Also accept the possibility of bias within the experiment eg 'The pupils might throw them wrongly.' 'Thrown by different people, different ways.' However, **do not accept** indication that the dice are biased; the question states they are fair. **Do not accept** irrelevant information eg 'The pupils didn't throw them the same amount of times.' **Do not accept** a restatement of the question, or that theory and practice are not linked, or that one set of results is an estimate of the other eg 'Theoretical results different from practical.' 'Pupil results are real, others are theory.' 'Theoretical results are only estimates.'
2m	e	**For 2m** indicates a correct probability eg ■ $\frac{1}{1296}$ ■ '0.00077' ■ '7.716×10^{-4}' ■ '0.077%' **For 1m** indicates a correct probability using the pupils' data from part (a) or the appropriate value from the second table in part (c) eg ■ $\frac{81}{90000}$ ■ $\frac{9}{10000}$ ■ '0.0009' ■ $\frac{8}{300} \times \frac{8}{300} = \frac{4}{5625}$ or Shows a correct method using either set of data or the probability from part (c) eg ■ $\frac{1}{36} \times \frac{1}{36}$ or $\frac{9}{300} \times \frac{9}{300}$ or $\frac{8}{300} \times \frac{8}{300}$ ■ '0.027^2' or '0.03 × 0.03' or '0.0266^2'	**For 2m** provided there is not an incorrect method, accept equivalent fractions, decimals or percentages which are rounded to 1 or more s.f. or truncated to 2 or more s.f.

61

Marks		Question 21	Sailing
		Correct response	**Additional guidance**
2m	a	**For 2m** indicates a value between 8.9(0) and 8.91 inclusive. **For only 1m** shows a complete correct method eg ■ '$\sqrt{(4.8^2 + 7.5^2)}$' ■ '$\sqrt{79.29}$' ■ '$\sqrt{79}$' ■ '$\tan^{-1} 7.5 \div 4.8 = 57.3, 7.5 \div \sin 57.3$' ■ '$4.8 \div \cos 57.4$'	*Throughout the question* do **not** accept answers found through scale or scaled drawings. **For 2m** accept 9 only if a correct value or correct working is seen. **For 1m** if Pythagoras is used, the intent to square both, add and square root must be shown, even if there are computational errors. **Do not accept** 79(.29....) without the intent to square root shown or implied.
2m	b	**For 2m** indicates a value between (0)56 and (0)56.5 inclusive eg ■ '056' ■ '56' **For only 1m** shows a correct method eg ■ '$\tan \theta = 6 \div 4$' ■ '$\tan^{-1} \dfrac{6}{4}$' ■ '$6^2 + 4^2 = 7.2^2, \cos x = 4 \div 7.2$' ■ '$\sin = 6 \div 7.211$' ■ '$\dfrac{6}{\sin \theta} = \dfrac{7.2}{\sin 90}$'	Ignore any subsequent correction for magnetic north. For 1m **do not accept** a wrong method, eg '$\tan \theta = 4 \div 6$' unless it is clear, eg by labelling on the diagram or subsequent subtraction from 90°, that the angle referred to is the one at Bargate. If this angle is then correctly found as between (0)33.5 and (0)34 inclusive, award **1m**.

Marks		Question 21 (cont)	Sailing (cont)
		Correct response	**Additional guidance**
3m	c	For **3m** indicates a value between 1.4(0) and 1.41 inclusive. For only **2m** shows the total distance north is a value between 5.4(0) and 5.41 inclusive. **or** Shows a complete correct method for the distance north of Bargate eg ■ '6 ÷ tan 48 − 4' ■ '6 × tan 42 − 4' 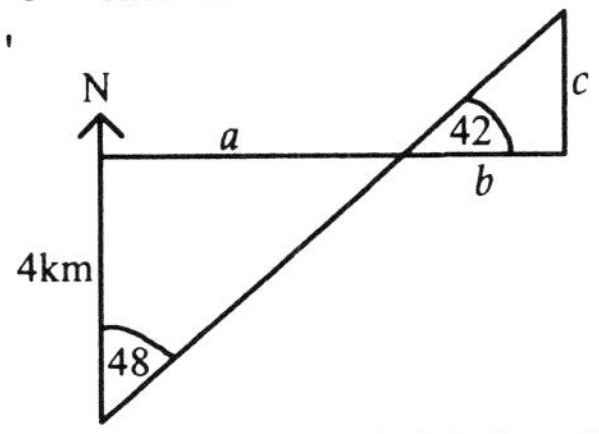 ■ ' $a = \tan 48 \times 4 = 4.44$, $b = 6 - 4.44 = 1.56$ $c = \tan 42 \times 1.56$' ■ '$\dfrac{d}{\sin 8.3} = \dfrac{7.21}{\sin 48}$' ■ '$x \div \sin 8 = 7.21 \div \sin 48$' For only **1m** shows a correct method for finding the total distance north eg ■ '6 ÷ tan 48' ■ '6 × tan 42' **or** Using the sine rule, makes one error eg ■ '$x \div \sin 8 = 7.21 \div \sin 56$' **or** Using similar triangles, makes one error or correctly finds the values of a and b as shown above.	

Marks		Question 22	Births
		Correct response	**Additional guidance**

2m	a	**For 2m** indicates 13 or 13.0(.....)
		
		For only 1m shows a complete correct method with not more than one computational error
		eg
		■ '17.6 – (26.1 ÷ 100 × 17.6)'
		■ '73.9 ÷ 100 × 17.6'
		■ '0.739 × 17.6'
		■ '(100 – 26.1) ÷ 100 × 17.6'
		■ '0.176 × 26.1 = 4.59, 17.6 – 4.59'
		or
		Shows a value between 4.5 and 4.6 inclusive
		eg
		■ '4.5936'
			Accept a correct response written within the table even if an incorrect or partial response is shown on the answer line.
			
			Accept a value expressed as a rate
			eg
			    '13 in 1000'
			    '13/1000'
			
			For 1m **do not accept** a description of the process
			eg
			    '17.6 – 26.1%'
			The method must show how this is to be evaluated.
			
			Do not accept incorrect methods
			eg
			    $\frac{17.6}{1.261}$

2m	b	**For 2m** indicates 28 or a value between 28.2 and 28.3 inclusive. **For only 1m** shows a complete correct method eg ■ '(17.0 - 12.2) ÷ 17' ■ '4.8 ÷ 17' ■ '12.2 ÷ 17 × 100 = 71.76, 100 – 71.76' ■ '17 – 12.2 = 5, 5 ÷ 17 = 0.294 = 29.4%' **or** Shows a correct partial method to find 12.2 as a percentage of 17.0 eg ■ '12.2 ÷ 17' ■ '71.8%'	Accept as evidence a value between 71.7 and 72 inclusive.
1m	c	Indicates the third statement eg ■	Accept any indication.

Marks		Question 23	Trees
		Correct response	**Additional guidance**
1m	a	Indicates the median is a value between 0.62 and 0.63 inclusive.	
2m		**For 2m** indicates the interquartile range is a value between 0.07 and 0.1(0) inclusive.	
		For only 1m shows a correct method to find the two quartiles eg ■ Draws vertical lines on the grid, corresponding to the quartiles. ■ Shows on the *x*-axis marks or values corresponding to the quartiles. or Indicates the values of the 2 quartiles but does not process them or processes them incorrectly eg ■ '0.57, 0.67'	The quartiles need not be accurate provided the intention to position them corresponding to half way between the 25 and 50 marks, and half way between the 100 and 125 marks, is clear. **Do not accept** quartiles indicated only by marks on the *y*-axis.
1m	b	Indicates the bottom left diagram eg ■	Accept any indication.

Mark Scheme Paper 2

Marks		Question 24	PLant Pots
		Correct response	**Additional guidance**
2m	a	**For 2m** indicates 28 **For only 1m** shows a correct ratio or a complete correct method eg • $\frac{m}{42} = \frac{40}{60}$ • $\frac{42}{m} = \frac{60}{40}$ • $\frac{40}{60} \times 42$ • 'It's $\frac{2}{3}$' • '42 ÷ 3 × 2' • '40 × 1.5 = 60, 42 ÷ 1.5'	
3m	a	**For 3m** indicates a value between 77.5 and 78 inclusive. **For only 2m** shows a correct substitution and evaluation eg • A value between 77500 and 78000 inclusive. **For only 1m** shows or implies a correct substitution and evaluation of the component parts of $a^2 + ab + b^2$ eg • Shows in working any of the values 7056, 24696, 296352, 931017.2(....) • Shows in working '3600 + 2160 + 1296'	**For 2m** accept as evidence the digits 775.... to 780.... eg '7.76'
1m	c	Gives a correct explanation eg • 'Volume factor is scale factor cubed.' • '$(\frac{2}{3})^3 = \frac{8}{27}$' • '2 × 2 × 2 = 8, 3 × 3 × 3 = 27' **or** Calculates the capacity of the smaller pot, using a value of 24 for the base, to show that the ratio applies.	**Do not accept** partial or incorrect explanations eg 'It's increased not just for the width, but also for the height and length as well.' '40 is a third off 60, and 8 is about a third of 27' 'Volume ratio is linear ratio squared.' The capacity of the smaller pot is approximately 23000cm³. However, since this value can be found by the capacity of the larger pot ÷ 27 × 8, **do not accept** this value unless it is clear it has been worked from first principles.

Mental arithmetic tests 1998
Transcripts and
Mark Scheme

[Blank page]

Additional guidance on administering and marking the mental arithmetic tests

Your child should have only a pen or pencil. He or she should not have erasers, rulers, calculators or any other mathematical equipment. Access to paper for working out answers is **not allowed.**

Give your child the answer sheet and ask him or her to write their name and school in the box at the top of the answer sheet. The answer sheets are in the pocket on the inside back cover of this book.

Ensure your child understands that:

- he or she will be told how long there is to answer each question and that the time given will increase from 5, to 10, to 15 seconds, as the test progresses through the three sections;

- for some of the questions, the information needed is included in or beside the answer box on the answer sheet;

- he or she is not allowed to use a calculator or any other mathematical equipment;

- to change an answer, he or she should put a cross through the first answer. He or she is not allowed to rub out any answers;

- he or she should answer as many questions as possible. If a question is too difficult, he or she should put a cross in the answer box, and wait for the next question;

- he or she must not ask any questions once the test has started;

- the small box to the right of each answer box is for marking the test.

General guidance for markers

Please note that your child should not be penalised if he or she records any information given in the question or shows any working. Ignore any annotation, even if in the answer space, and mark only the answer. Accept an unambiguous answer written in the stimulus box, or elsewhere on the page.

The general guidance for the marking of the written tests also applies to the marking of the mental arithmetic tests. In addition, please apply the following principles:

Unless specific instructions to the contrary are given in the mark scheme:

- accept responses written in words and/or figures,
    eg, 7 point 3, 4 hundred;

- accept any unambiguous indication of the correct response from a given list,
    eg, circling, ticking, underlining;

- accept unambiguous misspellings;

- accept units that have been correctly converted to a different unit provided the new unit is indicated. Where units are specified and given on the answer sheet, do not penalise pupils for writing in the units again;

- accept any unambiguous indication of a specific time,
    eg, 08:20, 8:20, 0820, 8.20, 08-20am, 20 minutes after 8.

The following script is the introduction to the test which is read at the beginning

Listen carefully to the instructions I am going to give you. When I have finished reading them, I will stop the tape and will answer any questions.
However, you will not be able to ask any questions once the test has begun.

I will start by reading a practice question. Then I am going to ask you 30 questions for the test. On your sheet there is an answer box for each question, where you should write the answer to the question and nothing else. You should work out the answer to each question in your head, but you may jot things down outside the answer box if this helps you. Do not try to write down your calculations because this will waste time and you may miss the next question. For some of the questions, important information is already written down for you on the sheet.

I will read out each question twice. Listen carefully both times. You will then have time to work out your answer. If you cannot work out an answer, put a cross in the answer box. If you make a mistake, cross out the wrong answer and write the correct answer next to it. There are some easy and some harder questions, so don't be put off if you cannot answer a question.

I will now *answer any questions you might have.*

Here is the practice question to show you what to do. I will read the question twice, and you will have five seconds to work out the answer and write it in the answer box.

What is half of fifty? (Lower tier Test C)

Subtract sixteen point four from seventeen point eight. (Higher tiers Tests A and B)

(The question is repeated)

What is half of fifty? (Lower tier Test C)

Subtract sixteen point four from seventeen point eight. (Higher tiers Tests A and B)

(Five second pause)

Now put down your pens.

Lower tier Test C questions

"Now we are ready to start the test.
For this first group of questions you will have 5 seconds to work out each answer and write it down."

	The Questions:	Pupil Sheet	
1	Imagine two squares that are the same size. Imagine you join them together side by side. What is the name of the new shape you have made?		
2	Write the number two thousand and twenty-eight in figures.		
3	How many centimetres are there in one metre?	cm	
4	Write a number that is bigger than twenty-eight and a half but less than twenty-nine.		
5	What is nine multiplied by seven?		
6	Look at the equation on your answer sheet. What is the value of two y?		$6y = 66$
7	What is seven hundred and thirty-two divided by one hundred?		732

"For the next group of questions you will have 10 seconds to work out each answer and write it down."

	The Questions:	Pupil Sheet	
8	What is the cost of four birthday cards at one pound and five pence each?	£	
9	Your answer sheet shows three scores in a darts game. What is the total score?		18 7 12
10	Look at the spinners on your answer sheet. Tick the spinner which is most likely to land on grey.		
11	Look at the equation on your answer sheet. What is the value of n?		$21 - n = 8$
12	What number is one hundred less than eight thousand? Write your answer in figures.		
13	The pie chart on your answer sheet shows how a group of pupils travel to school. Approximately what percentage of these pupils cycle to school?	%	
14	Look at the squares on your answer sheet. How many small squares will fit inside the larger square?		
15	A jacket costs fifty-two pounds. In a sale the price is nineteen pounds less. What is the sale price?	£	£52 £19

"Now turn over your answer sheet."

4

Lower tier Test C questions

(10 second questions continued)

	The Questions:	Pupil Sheet	
16	A pen costs three pounds forty-nine. I buy two pens. How much change do I get from ten pounds?	£	£3.49
17	How many hours is three hundred minutes?	hours	
18	Subtract twenty from eight.		
19	The perimeter of an equilateral triangle is thirty centimetres. What is the length of each side?	cm	30cm
20	A famous author lived in a house from eighteen eighty-seven to nineteen twenty. For how long did she live there?	years	1887 1920
21	Look at the calculation on your answer sheet. Work out the answer.		30 ÷ (6 − 3)
22	Look at the measurements on your answer sheet. Which one is about the same length as five miles? Circle your answer.	4km 8km 12km 16km	
23	A skirt cost thirty pounds. The price went up by ten percent. What is the new price?	£	£30

"For the next group of questions you will have 15 seconds to work out each answer and write it down."

	The Questions:	Pupil Sheet	
24	One of the shapes on your answer sheet has no lines of symmetry. Put a tick inside this shape.	○ ▱ △ ⬠	
25	Look at the timetable on your answer sheet. How long does the journey take from Tarn to Barham?	minutes	Holt 10:28 Calne 10:33 Tarn 10:38 Priory 10:41 Barham 10:45 Armill 10:47
26	Imagine a square, cut out of paper. Put a ring around two shapes you could make by folding the square in half.	circle rectangle square rhombus triangle	
27	Look at the numbers on your answer sheet. Put a circle around the smallest number.	0.2 0.1 0.28 0.23 0.02	
28	Use the calculation on your answer sheet to help you work out the answer to one hundred and forty-four divided by six.		144 ÷ 3 = 48
29	Imagine a solid cone, standing on its circular base. Cut the cone in half, from top to bottom. What is the shape of the vertical face made by the cut?		
30	What is the next prime number after twenty-three?		

"Put your pens down. The test is finished."

5

Key Stage 3 Mathematics 1998
Mental Arithmetic Lower Tier Test C

Test C

Mark Scheme

Accept alternative terms for possible shapes, eg oblong, domino, octagon. Do not accept 3-D shapes, eg cuboid. Do not accept drawn responses without indication of the name.

Time: 5 seconds

1	**rectangle**	SEE ABOVE.

2	**2028**	Accept correct digits with commas as spacers, eg 2,028. Do not accept incorrect use of decimal points, eg 202.8. Do not accept responses given in words.

3	**100** cm	

4	**28.5 < answer < 29**	eg 28.6, 28¾

5	**63**	

6	**22**	

7	**7.32**	Accept equivalent fractions or decimals. Do not accept remainders, eg 7r32.

Time: 10 seconds

8	**£ 4.20**	

9	**37**	

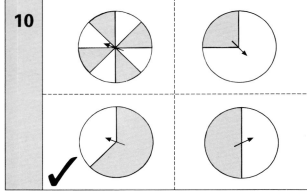

10	

11	**13**	

12	**7900**	Accept correct digits with commas as spacers, eg 7,900. Do not accept incorrect use of decimal points, eg 79.00. Do not accept responses given in words.

13	**23 % ≤ answer ≤ 27 %**	eg 25%

14	**9**	Do not accept drawn responses without indication of 9.

15	**£ 33**	

Lower tier Test C mark scheme continued

16	£ 3.02	

17	**5** hours	

18	**–12**	

19	**10** cm	Accept more than one of the sides given.

20	**33** years	SEE RIGHT.

Also accept indication that, as well as 33, 32 or 34 could be possible, eg 32 to 33, 33-34, 32 to 34.

21	**10**	

22	4km (8km) 12km 16km	

23	£ **33**	Do not accept redundant % signs, eg 33%

Ignore extra information such as equilateral. Also accept drawings of triangles, provided no side is drawn as a curve.

Time: 15 seconds

24	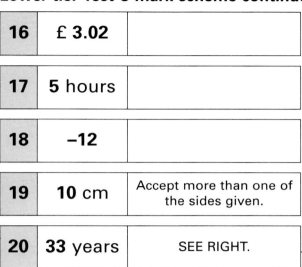

25	**7** minutes	

26	circle (rectangle) square rhombus (triangle)

27	0.2 0.1 0.28 0.23 (0.02)

28	**24**	

29	**triangle**	SEE ABOVE.

30	**29**	

Higher tiers Test A questions

"Now we are ready to start the test.
For this first group of questions you will have 5 seconds to work out each answer and write it down."

	The Questions:	Pupil Sheet	
1	What is thirty-seven multiplied by ten?		
2	Write one quarter as a decimal.		
3	There are four red cubes and six blue cubes in a bag. I choose a cube at random. What is the probability that I choose a blue cube?		4 red 6 blue
4	How many metres are there in two and a half kilometres?	m	

"For the next group of questions you will have 10 seconds to work out each answer and write it down."

	The Questions:	Pupil Sheet	
5	Look at the calculation on your answer sheet. Work out the answer.		$7 \times (3 + 4)$
6	What is five point four added to three point seven?		5.4 3.7
7	Twenty-five per cent of a number is twelve. What is the number?		
8	Look at the expression on your answer sheet. Its value is eighty-two. Write an expression with a value of forty-one.		$4k + 2n$ 82
9	Write another fraction that is equivalent to three fifths.		$\dfrac{3}{5}$
10	Look at the triangle on your answer sheet. What is the area of this triangle?	cm²	
11	Look at the equation on your answer sheet. If m equals six, what is h?	$h =$	$h = \dfrac{7m}{2}$
12	Look at the equation on your answer sheet. Write what number x could be.		$x^2 = x$
13	Look at the equation on your answer sheet. What is the value of n?		$26 - 2n = 8$
14	In a country, the probability that it will rain in August is nought point nought five. What is the probability that it will not rain in August?		0.05
15	Assume a person's heart beats seventy times in one minute. How many times will it beat in one hour?		70

"Now turn over your answer sheet."

8

Higher tiers Test A questions

	The Questions:	Pupil Sheet	
16	The mean of a, b and c is ten. a is six. b is eleven. What is c?	$c =$	10 $a = 6$ $b = 11$
17	Look at the expression on your answer sheet. Multiply out this expression.		$3y(y + 6)$
18	Write an approximate answer to the calculation on your answer sheet.		$\dfrac{50.6}{0.49}$

"For the next group of questions you will have 15 seconds to work out each answer and write it down."

	The Questions:	Pupil Sheet	
19	Arrange the digits three, five and two to make the largest possible odd number.		3 5 2
20	Look at the lengths on your answer sheet. Put a circle around the median length.	820m 620m 430m 560m 550m	
21	Use the calculation on your answer sheet to help you work out the answer to fourteen multiplied by three point nine.		$14 \times 39 = 546$
22	What is eighteen multiplied by nine?		18
23	Imagine a robot moving so that it is always the same distance from a fixed point. Describe the shape of the path the robot makes.		
24	Two of the angles in a triangle are forty-seven degrees and eighty-five degrees. How many degrees is the other angle?	degrees	47 85
25	The sum of p and q is twelve. The product of p and q is twenty-seven. What are the values of p and q?	...... and	12 27
26	Seventy-five miles per hour is about the same as thirty-three metres per second. About how many metres per second is fifty miles per hour?	m/s	75mph 33m/s 50mph
27	Look at the net of a cube on your answer sheet. When you fold it up, which edge will meet edge A? Draw an arrow pointing to the correct edge.	A↓	
28	In a raffle, one half of the tickets are bought by men. One third are bought by women. The rest are bought by children. What fraction of the tickets are bought by children?		$\dfrac{1}{2}$ $\dfrac{1}{3}$
29	Multiply twenty-five by twenty-eight.		25 28
30	A cuboid has edges of three, four and five centimetres. Its volume is sixty cubic centimetres. What is the volume of a cuboid with edges that are twice as long?	cm³	3, 4, 5 60

"Put your pens down. The test is finished."

9

Key Stage 3 Mathematics 1998
Mental Arithmetic Higher Tiers Test A

Test A
Mark Scheme

Time: 5 seconds

1	370	
2	(0).25	Accept equivalent decimals only.
3	$\dfrac{6}{10}$	Accept equivalent probabilities.
4	2500 m	Accept correct digits with commas as spacers, eg 25,00. Do not accept incorrect use of decimal points, eg 2.500

Time: 10 seconds

5	49	
6	9.1	
7	48	Do not accept incorrect use of % signs, eg 48%
8	$2k + (1)n\ (= 41)$	Accept equivalent expressions, eg $\dfrac{4k + 2n}{2}$
9	Any fraction, or decimal, that is equivalent to $\dfrac{3}{5}$, eg 0.6, $\dfrac{6}{10}$, $\dfrac{30}{50}$	
10	30 cm^2	
11	$h = 21$	
12	**1** or **0** or both	
13	9	
14	(0).95	Accept equivalent probabilities.
15	4200	Accept correct digits with commas as spacers, eg 4,200. Do not accept incorrect use of decimal points, eg 420.0

Higher tiers Test A mark scheme continued

16	$c = 13$	

17	$3y^2 + 18y$	Do not accept incomplete processing, eg $3y^2 + 3 \times 6y$

18	$100 \leq$ **answer** ≤ 105	eg 100, 101.5.

Accept descriptions of the shape, eg circular. Accept unambiguous drawings.

Time: 15 seconds

19	**523**	

20	820m 620m 430m (560m) 550m	

21	**54.6**	

22	**162**	

23	**circle, sphere** or **hemisphere**	

24	**48** degrees	

25	**3** and **9**	Accept in either order.

26	$21 \leq$ **answer** ≤ 23 m/s	eg 22

Accept non-ambiguous responses, eg 3,9 or 3 9. Do not accept ambiguous responses, eg 39

27	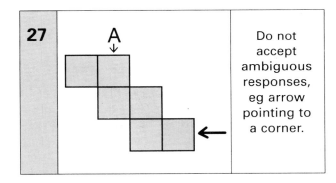	Do not accept ambiguous responses, eg arrow pointing to a corner.

28	$\dfrac{1}{6}$	Accept equivalent fractions or decimals.

29	**700**	

30	**480** cm^3	

Higher tiers Test B questions

"Now we are ready to start the test.
For this first group of questions you will have 5 seconds to work out each answer and write it down."

	The Questions:	Pupil Sheet	
1	What is sixty-three divided by nine?		
2	How many millilitres are there in a litre?	ml	
3	A quarter of a number is one point two five. What is the number?		1.25
4	I throw two dice. The probability that I get a total of eight is five thirty-sixths. What is the probability that I do not get a total of eight?		$\dfrac{5}{36}$

"For the next group of questions you will have 10 seconds to work out each answer and write it down."

	The Questions:	Pupil Sheet	
5	I spend two pounds twenty. How much change will I get from five pounds?	£	
6	Look at the measurements on your answer sheet. Which one is about the same length as one metre? Circle your answer.	0.3 feet 3 feet 30 feet 300 feet	
7	Pencils cost thirty-seven pence each. How many pencils can you buy with three pounds seventy?	£3.70	
8	Two angles fit together to make a straight line. One angle is eighty-six degrees. How many degrees is the other angle?	degrees	
9	Thirty-five per cent of a number is forty-two. What is seventy per cent of the number?	35% 42	
10	Look at the cuboid on your answer sheet. What is the volume of this cuboid?	cm³	4cm 3cm 2cm
11	Four out of fifty pupils were absent from school. What percentage of pupils were absent?	% 4 50	
12	What is five point one multiplied by one thousand?	5.1	
13	Imagine a regular square-based pyramid. Imagine another identical pyramid. Stick their square faces together. How many faces does your new shape have?		
14	Look at the calculation on your answer sheet. Write down the answer.	$\dfrac{34.2}{2.8 + 7.2}$	
15	Rearrange the equation on your answer sheet to make b the subject of the equation.	$b =$	$a = \dfrac{b}{c}$

"Now turn over your answer sheet."

12

Higher tiers Test B questions

(10 second questions continued)

	The Questions:	Pupil Sheet	
16	Write in figures the number that is one less than seven and a half million.		
17	Imagine two trees. Now imagine walking so that you are always an equal distance from each tree. Describe the shape of the path that you walk.		
18	The probability that a train will be late is nought point three. Of fifty trains, about how many would you expect to be late?		0.3 50

"For the next group of questions you will have 15 seconds to work out each answer and write it down."

	The Questions:	Pupil Sheet	
19	Look at the dots on your answer sheet. Four of the dots are at the corners of a square. Join the four dots to make a square.		(pattern of dots)
20	The pie chart on your answer sheet shows how two hundred pupils travel to school. Roughly how many of these pupils cycle to school?		(pie chart: Car, Cycle, Bus, Walk)
21	What is one hundred and twenty-eight multiplied by five?		128
22	Use the calculation on your answer sheet to help you work out the answer to four hundred and sixty-eight divided by fifteen.		$234 \div 15 = 15.6$
23	Estimate the value of five hundred and two divided by forty-nine.		502 49
24	Carpet tiles are fifty centimetres by fifty centimetres. How many do you need to cover one square metre?		50cm
25	Look at the equation on your answer sheet. If c equals eight, what is d?	$d =$	$d^2 = 2c + 9$
26	A square has an area of t squared. What is the perimeter of the square?		t^2
27	x equals two and y equals three. Work out the value of x to the power y plus y to the power x.		$x = 2$ $y = 3$ $x^y + y^x$
28	Look at the calculation on your answer sheet. Write an approximate answer.		$\dfrac{103 \times 0.44}{\sqrt{16.1}}$
29	Look at the equation on your answer sheet. Write an expression, in terms of t, for m plus five.		$m + 7 = t$
30	On your answer sheet are two numbers. Write the number which is half way between them.		$3\frac{2}{5}$ 4

"Put your pens down. The test is finished."

Key Stage 3 Mathematics 1998
Mental Arithmetic Higher Tiers Test B

Test B
Mark Scheme

Time: 5 seconds

1	7	
2	**1000** ml	Accept correct digits with commas as spacers, eg 10,00. Do not accept incorrect use of decimal points, eg 1.000
3	5	Accept equivalent numbers, eg 5.0, 5.00
4	$\frac{31}{36}$	Accept equivalent probabilities.

Time: 10 seconds

5	£ 2.80	
6	0.3 feet ③ feet 30 feet 300 feet	
7	10	
8	**94** degrees	Accept correct values even if written on the wrong angle.
9	84	Do not accept incorrect use of % signs, eg 84%
10	**24** cm³	
11	**8** %	
12	**5100**	Accept correct digits with commas as spacers, eg 51,00. Do not accept incorrect use of decimal points, eg 5.100
13	8	Also accept 10
14	**3.42**	
15	$b = ac$	

Higher tiers Test B mark scheme continued

16	7 499 999	Accept correct digits with commas as spacers, eg 749,999,9. Do not accept incorrect use of decimal points, eg 7.499.999. Do not accept responses given in words.
17	(straight) line	SEE OPPOSITE. →
18	15	Also accept any range between 12 and 18 that includes 15, or indication that 15 is approximate, eg about 15

Accept equivalent words or phrases, eg bisector, straight, perpendicular to the line between the trees. Accept unambiguous drawings, eg

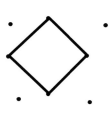

Do not accept ambiguous responses, eg parallel, through the middle of the trees. Do not accept an incorrect response alongside a correct response, eg straight and parallel.

Time: 15 seconds

19		Accept any indication of the correct 4 points, even if the lines are not straight or have not been drawn.
20	$45 \leq$ **answer** ≤ 55	Do not accept incorrect use of % signs, eg 50%
21	640	
22	31.2	
23	$10 \leq$ **answer** ≤ 11	eg 10, 10.3

24	4	
25	$d =$ **5** or **− 5** or both	
26	**4t**	Accept equivalent expressions, eg $t + t + t + t$, $2t + 2t$
27	17	Do not accept incomplete processing, eg 8 + 9
28	$10 \leq$ **answer** ≤ 13	
29	$(m + 5 =)\ t - 2$	
30	**3.7** or $3\frac{7}{10}$ or equivalent	

END OF TEST

Printed in the United Kingdom for The Stationery Office
J71825 C20 2/99 9385 9829